PHILOSOPHICAL TASKS

Philosophy

─────

Editor

PROFESSOR S. KÖRNER
jur.Dr., Ph.D., F.B.A.

Professor of Philosophy
University of Bristol and Yale University

PHILOSOPHICAL TASKS

AN INTRODUCTION TO SOME AIMS AND METHODS
IN RECENT PHILOSOPHY

Graham Bird

Professor of Philosophy
University of Stirling

HUTCHINSON UNIVERSITY LIBRARY
LONDON

HUTCHINSON & CO (*Publishers*) LTD
3 Fitzroy Square, London W1

London Melbourne Sydney Auckland
Wellington Johannesburg Cape Town
and agencies throughout the world

First published 1972

*This book has been set in Times type, printed in Great Britain
on smooth wove paper by Anchor Press, and
bound by Wm. Brendon, both of Tiptree, Essex*

ISBN 0 09 113250 9 (cased)
0 09 113251 7 (paper)

To LOUISE, COLIN and MICHAEL

CONTENTS

PREFACE

My intention has been to produce a book that might introduce readers to some aspects of recent Anglo-American philosophy. Several books have outlined the development of philosophy up to the beginnings of so-called linguistic philosophy. Some books have been extremely critical of this latest development. I have tried to introduce readers to arguments and material which would enable them to reach some view of these developments for themselves.

I would like to thank the editor of the series, Professor Körner, and the publishers for their heroic patience, my philosophical colleagues at Stirling and my family for their cooperation, and Ieuan Williams for help with the bibliography.

G.H.B.

Dollar, 1972

I

THE REVOLUTIONARY BACKGROUND

1. *Introduction*

Philosophers have always been concerned with method. Some, like Kant, have been very interested in it; and some, like Descartes, have been almost obsessed by it. Sometimes they have been eager to raise and discuss questions of method, as these two philosophers were; but sometimes, particularly recently, they have been equally eager to avoid such questions. Sometimes they have wanted to consider the methods of the established sciences, and sometimes they have wanted to consider the methods of philosophy itself. And sometimes, particularly in traditional philosophy, they have failed to distinguish these different interests. Sometimes, again, they have wanted to *recommend* particular methods, whether for philosophy or for other disciplines; but sometimes they have wanted only to *describe* the methods employed for some particular task.

All these interests, though concerned with method, are concerned with it in very different ways. There can, for these and other reasons, be no presumption that two philosophers concerned with questions of method are interested in exactly the same thing. To notice these initial complexities in what may seem a simple idea is to take a necessary first step away from the term's hypnotic influence. It is to begin to be immune to some of the infections which the idea of 'method' has undoubtedly carried. And it is all the more necessary for me to offer some such safeguard, since I have chosen to introduce an account of recent philosophy in terms of its aims and methods. One powerful reason for such a choice lies in the common claim that there has been a revolution in philosophy in recent times, and that as a consequence its aims and methods have radically changed.[1]

[1] See, for example, A. J. Ayer *et al.*, *The Revolution in Philosophy* (London, 1956).

Any attempt to understand the nature of philosophical tasks nowadays must begin with some examination of these revolutionary ideas.

First, however, it is important to notice the resistance sometimes offered to such a discussion of method in philosophy. The slogan 'Don't talk about philosophy, do some' has sometimes itself seemed to be a part of the revolution. And if it were, then there would be at least one good reason for disregarding it. For such a slogan withdraws the revolutionary methods both from discussion and, except accidentally, from change. But it is a background principle in philosophy to exempt nothing from discussion, as it is also a general principle of revolution that nothing is exempt from change. It is, of course, notorious that revolutions in the end betray their principles, so that the desire to consolidate a reform may come to outweigh the desire for change itself. It is natural that revolutionaries should believe that they know the right things to do and the proper way to do them, but that is no good reason to exempt their beliefs from discussion. To say 'Don't talk about philosophy, do some' is to assume that the tasks, the aims and methods, of philosophy are finally established beyond question. Yet these beliefs always can, and sometimes should, be questioned.

It is, nevertheless, true that such questioning is worth while only if it can be brought into contact with particular philosophical problems. The slogan, for which in general there is little to be said, rightly acknowledges the futility of a certain kind of interest in method. Very often the chess player who likes to discuss endlessly the theoretical advantages or disadvantages of an opening variation will turn out to be a poor player over the board. He forgets that the test of such theoretical appraisal lies in the outcome in practical play. A scientist who prefers idle speculation to careful measurement may mask his preference as an interest in method. An exclusive interest in method may develop uselessly into an interest in methodology. But if such interests have their dangers it would still be needlessly pessimistic to give them up altogether. In recognising a trap we are in part protected from it. The usual procedure in philosophy has been to undertake a particular task and to let the reader draw his own conclusions about the methods employed in tackling it. There need be no harm, and may be some benefit, in becoming for a time rather more self-conscious than usual about the latter.

There is another, more detailed, set of reasons for disregarding the slogan. What we regard as the tasks of philosophy cannot be independent of what we regard as its proper methods. What are thought of as properly philosophical methods will determine, or be determined by, what are thought of as legitimate philosophical tasks. Methods and tasks, of course, go hand in hand; in choosing philosophical methods we are already identifying philosophical tasks. But in many ways the revolution in philosophy rested upon the advocacy of new and distinctive techniques in the subject. It would be difficult, for example, to over-emphasise the importance in the revolution of the new methods of analysis offered by modern logic. And it is easy to see how, among logical positivists, new methods of attempting to separate what is meaningful from what is meaningless determined the approval or disapproval of certain traditional philosophical tasks. Even the most recently labelled development in the revolution, so-called linguistic philosophy, is said by a recent writer to be 'primarily the name of a method'.[1]

But the temptation to identify philosophy with a method, or set of methods, is even stronger than this suggests. At least one revolutionary philosopher, namely Wittgenstein, held that philosophy had no distinctive subject-matter, but was merely an activity of clarification. Such a view at least rules out one possible and traditional way of locating philosophical problems in terms of their topics. Plainly if Wittgenstein's view were right it would be only misleading to identify philosophical tasks in terms of any list of topics whether traditional or not. Such a list might illustrate areas in which philosophers had been interested, but it would fail to show what was distinctively philosophical about that interest. For that would depend not so much on the choice of a topic as on the way in which, in philosophy, the topic was handled; that is, it would depend on the distinctive methods which philosophers employ in their task of clarification.

Not all philosophers would agree with this view of Wittgenstein's, but it is important to recognise that it rests on more than a mere methodological prejudice. It is exceedingly hard to find any philosophical topic which is not also involved in other disciplines or practices. Moral philosophers are interested in rights and duties, in obligations, contracts, justice and responsibility. But these items form also part of the stock-in-trade of lawyers, politicians and divines. Epistemologists have an interest in memory and imagination, perception, belief and language; but so have psychologists, sociologists and linguists. To attempt to identify philosophical tasks in terms of such topics as these would be to fail to distinguish philosophy from other disciplines. Once again, if such a distinction is to be made it must rest not so much on a difference of topic as on a difference in the way in which the topics are treated. To say this

[1] J. Searle, *Speech Acts* (Cambridge, 1969), p. 4.

is at once to identify philosophy in terms of its methods. Although methods, tasks, and topics are inevitably linked, it seems that in the revolution philosophy is to be located primarily in terms of its method.

It was, for example, another fundamental doctrine in the revolution that the methods of philosophy and science are quite distinct. Such a view seems a natural corollary of the point just made. Where science and philosophy share an interest in the same topic any distinction between them will naturally reflect a difference in their approach to that topic. It may seem to follow from this that it would be quite wrong to expect from philosophers the answers to scientific questions, or to expect scientists and philosophers to offer rival answers to the same questions. Professor Peters, in a recent book, outlined the scope of his own philosophical discussion by drawing just such a contrast.

A scientific question, for instance, is one that can in principle be answered by certain kinds of procedures in which observation and experiment play a crucial part. But the clarification and discussion of the concepts used and of how they have meaning, and of the procedures by means of which these questions are answered, is a philosophical enquiry.[1]

Even where the distinction between philosophy and science is not explicitly invoked a similar contrast has often been drawn. Professor Berlin, for example, distinguishes a number of philosophical from non-philosophical questions where at least part of the difference is that in the latter cases there are clear and established procedures for providing answers even if the answers are not yet known.[2] One of his examples of a non-philosophical question is 'Have any ravens been seen in Iceland in 1955?', which a naturalist might be expected to answer decisively; and this is contrasted with the philosophical question 'Are there any material objects in the universe (or does it perhaps consist rather of minds and their states)?'. It may, of course, be doubted whether such an example helps to make clear the nature of philosophical questions. One might expect that most people who understood the questions would see only one difference between them, namely that whereas only a specialist might know the answer to the first question everyone knows already the answer to the second. Nevertheless this may seem in a roundabout way to confirm Berlin's point. For if one assumes that the philosophical question is genuine, then it may be thought to conceal a more profound problem whose solution is bafflingly obscure.

[1] R. S. Peters, *Ethics and Education* (London, 1966), p. 16.
[2] I. Berlin (Ed.), *The Age of Enlightenment* (New York, 1956), pp. 11–12.

The two quotations do not express exactly the same point. Berlin contrasts the presence of established methods for solving problems outside philosophy with their absence in philosophy itself; but he does not refer only to empirical methods, or only to methods employed in the sciences. Peters, on the other hand, contrasts philosophy and science, and apparently identifies scientific questions as those which can be answered by empirical methods. Both philosophers agree, however, that if a question can be answered by the empirical or observational procedures typical of the natural sciences, then it is not a philosophical question. Once again a general restriction on the legitimate methods of philosophy imposes also a restriction on its proper tasks. If we wish to consider what philosophy is or what it should be concerned with, then we cannot avoid some consideration of its methods.

This latter claim is especially true of the most recent developments of revolutionary philosophy. For these, as Peters' remarks about the clarification of concepts indicate, have been described in terms of a particular method involving language and its concepts. Certainly to talk barely of linguistic or conceptual clarification is to give a very general and over-simplified account of what its advocates would rightly regard as a complex set of techniques. Nevertheless it is in this area that the main difference between pre- and post-revolutionary philosophy is to be found. If there is one general label to mark this frontier and the new techniques which erected it, then the term 'linguistic' is the obvious candidate.

2. *Science and language*

So far I have considered quite generally some of the dangers to be avoided, and some of the reservations to be made, in talking of philosophical tasks and methods. But already two central features of recent philosophy have been noted in the claims, first that philosophy is quite different from science and employs quite different methods, and second that philosophy is concerned in some fundamental way with language and properly employs linguistic techniques. Both of these views will be examined in later chapters. For the present it is enough to disclose some of their supporting assumptions and some of the connections between them. What follows must rely to some extent on the way in which the revolution developed historically, but here there is no claim either to a comprehensive survey of that history or to accurate detail in its documentation.[1]

[1] For such historical and detailed treatment see J. O. Urmson, *Philosophical Analysis* (Oxford, 1956); or G. J. Warnock, *English Philosophy since 1900* (Oxford, 1963); or Ayer, op. cit.

As a start it should certainly be noted that the contrast between philosophy and science is of primary concern only to that part of philosophy which deals with theoretical claims and is generally called theory of knowledge. In all or most other parts of philosophy, in moral philosophy or aesthetics or political philosophy for example, there is no obvious science with which to contrast philosophical questions. Nevertheless even in these areas there are comparable contrasts to be drawn which help to show a more general principle involved in the revolution. Just as philosophers investigating claims to knowledge look naturally to the sciences for illustrations of those claims, so moral or political philosophers look, not perhaps to any science, but to some body of doctrine, some set of beliefs or code of practices for their material. In this way the contrast between philosophy and science appears only as an instance of a more profound distinction between philosophy and a whole range of other activities.

This more general distinction is sometimes put by referring to a difference in the level or order of these activities. First-floor disciplines and their practitioners deal with ground-floor phenomena. Philosophy as a second-order activity deals with the claims made in the first-order disciplines about the ground-floor phenomena. Parents, teachers, moral reformers, and indeed anybody engaged in ordinary moral thinking, issue views about what at ground-floor level ought to be done. In issuing such views they offer to philosophers material for analysis, and such analysis is a higher-level, second-order, activity one stage further removed from the ground-floor situations themselves. This, at any rate, was the theory. It has often been criticised in recent times, especially by non-philosophers and in moral contexts. To such critics it has seemed unfortunate, even irresponsible, that philosophers should insulate their tasks from substantial, ground-floor, moral issues by taking refuge in a morally neutral second-order analysis. Of course such a criticism tacitly concedes that a second-order analysis must be insulated from ground-floor issues, though probably few philosophers in the revolution would have accepted such an assumption without some qualification. Nevertheless some philosophers have wanted to defend such an assumption.[1]

The doctrine which separates philosophy in this way from ordinary first-order enquiries had a large part of its origin in modern logic. In formulating a logical system it is important to distinguish the expressions used in the system from claims that may be made about those expressions. If the expressions used in the system are said to form an object language, then claims made about those

[1] See Warnock, op. cit.

expressions form a higher order meta-language. Theoretical benefits may be conferred by investigating such a system with the help of meta-linguistic devices, and systematic traps may be avoided if the distinction between the two language levels is carefully adhered to.[1] It is not difficult to see the extension of this distinction from a formal, deductive, context to the wider sphere of philosophy itself in the doctrine that philosophy as a whole is a second-order activity.

Nor is it hard to see how such a doctrine, with such an origin, leads naturally to the view that philosophy is concerned mainly with language; that it is, properly speaking, a linguistic enquiry. For in the logical distinction out of which the doctrine grew the claims in the meta-language are simply claims about the expressions employed in the object language. Although perhaps the view that philosophy is a second-order activity does not *entail* that it is concerned with language, such a background provides a strong presumption, and equally strong temptation to believe, that it is. Expressed strictly with the rigour and care which modern logic demands philosophical assertions will always appear as claims about the expressions of a language, whether formal or natural. And, properly understood, philosophical questions similarly are really questions about such expressions, however much they may look like questions of fact. It was indeed an important part of the early revolution to claim that previous philosophers had been badly misled through failing to grasp the real force of their questions, or of the answers they had given to them. For earlier philosophers had expressed those questions and answers in the 'material' mode, or in the object language, which made it appear that the issues concerned ground-floor phenomena. In order to prevent such mistakes philosophers were urged to rephrase their questions in the 'formal' mode, with the help of meta-linguistic devices, in which the true nature of the issues was revealed to be linguistic.

Instead of asking whether God created the natural numbers philosophers were invited to put the question 'Are the natural number symbols *primitive* expressions in the language of mathematics?' Instead of saying 'Numbers are classes of things' it was thought better to say 'It is more fruitful and expedient (for certain purposes) to work with a language system in which numerical expressions are class expressions of the second level'.[2] In a less

[1] See, for example, W. V. O. Quine, *Mathematical Logic* (Harvard, 1940).
[2] For the original distinction between formal and material modes see R. Carnap, *Logical Syntax of Language* (London, 1937). The second illustration is from Y. Bar-Hillel, 'Carnap's Logical Syntax of Language' in P. Schilpp (Ed.), *The Philosophy of R. Carnap* (La Salle, 1963), p. 537.

technical context Berlin's question about the existence of material objects might be reformulated as a question about the value or function of the expression 'material object' in a language. It is clear that the reformulated questions may be importantly different from the originals. Certainly we may ask about the function of many words in a language without committing ourselves to the existence of some corresponding item in the world. In such obvious cases as the logical particles (words like 'if' and 'not'), or certain problematic terms (like 'luck' or 'fate'), we may not know the answer to the material question, or not even wish to raise it, even though an answer to its formal counterpart can be given.

These two central doctrines in the revolution naturally reinforced each other. The doctrine of the two levels encouraged the belief that philosophy had to do with language. The belief that philosophy was primarily concerned with language and not with fact, or with any ground-floor phenomenon, helped to deepen the division between the two levels. The combined influence of these doctrines leads naturally enough to the interposition of an insulating seal between philosophy and other first-order disciplines of the kind implicit in the quotation from Peters. But even if these views were accepted they would still tell us very little about the nature of philosophical interest in the languages of science, political belief, or moral conduct. And as a matter of history there were disagreements among philosophers as to the nature of this interest. All revolutionaries accepted a close link between philosophy and language, but they tended to disagree about the tasks to be performed on the various languages. In indicating some of these disagreements, or divergences of interest, we shall unearth some of the subsidiary ideas involved in the revolution.

It might have been expected that all revolutionaries would rally to the slogan of analysis, for certainly the term was, and still is, widely used to describe philosophical activity. But any such unanimity would have been only apparent, for the term by no means meant the same to all who used it. Moore, for example, certainly put analysis at the very centre of his own philosophical activity, and referred to Russell's theory of descriptions as a model of analysis. If the logical positivists had had to choose one phrase to describe their method they would surely have used the phrase 'logical analysis'. But Moore himself remained puzzled about the nature of his analytic activities, and certainly did not offer analyses of the same formal type as Russell's model. It would not be hard to accept Strawson's division between analysts, such as Russell and the logical positivists, whose techniques essentially involved formal logic, and others such as Moore, the later Wittgenstein, Ryle and Austin, for whom analysis was less systematic and not necessarily linked to the apparatus of formal logic.[1] But even this neat division certainly conceals differences, for example between Wittgenstein and Austin, or obscurities, for example about the characterisation of Moore's procedures. Despite these unclarities philosophers continue to identify their activities in terms of linguistic or conceptual analysis. Such descriptions function only as signposts to an understanding of philosophical tasks.

Philosophers in the revolution differed not only about the techniques to be employed, but also about the aims of their employment and the material on which they were to be used. In the light of what was said earlier about the link between tasks and methods it is not surprising, for example, that those philosophers for whom analysis necessarily involved formal logic should have had aims which were not shared by others who had no such requirement. The former would not be satisfied with anything less than a reformulation within a logical system, while the latter would not generally have wanted or expected such a result. But disagreement over aims was more serious than this. For some philosophers, especially logical positivists, the aim was the reconstruction in logical terms of the languages of the sciences. For others, especially Wittgenstein, the aim was the more limited and unsystematic eradication of mistakes which may arise from a misunderstanding even of ordinary language. For others, perhaps Austin and certainly Warnock, the aim was systematically to explore the conceptual features of ordinary language.

Associated with these differences of aim there are naturally differences in the location of the data of philosophy. For the logical positivists philosophy had as its data the languages of the sciences. For Wittgenstein philosophy certainly had no subject-matter, but was simply an activity of clarification or a therapy, which might be exercised on any obscure material. For Austin and Warnock philosophy has regained a topic, namely that of ordinary language. For them the task of philosophy is ultimately to give a systematic account not of the technical languages of science, but of the ordinary language used in everyday speech. It is easy to detect a common concern with language in all these accounts of philosophy. It is also easy to see that in all of them it is a distinct concern with different languages, or with different aspects of language.

[1] P. F. Strawson, 'Construction and Analysis' in *The Revolution in Philosophy*.

3. *Some problems*

These are, of course, no more than the bare outlines of philosophical positions, but they serve to locate some of the key notions and crucial difficulties in recent philosophy. At this stage it is worth while only to summarise briefly some of these ideas, and to indicate two general puzzles which they initially suggest.

First it has been noted how important is the idea of method in the philosophical revolution. It has often been claimed, for example, that the methods of science and philosophy must be quite distinct. While the former deals with its problems through established procedures of observation and experiment, the latter's problems cannot be treated in this way. Such an emphasis on the distinctive methods of philosophy may be reinforced by noting the revolutionary rejection of traditional topics, and by recognising that the things which have interested philosophers are almost always investigated in other disciplines as well. It may be still further reinforced by noticing the view held by some philosophers in the revolution that philosophy had no subject-matter but was merely a therapeutic activity of clarification.

Second, however, the division between science and philosophy is only a symptom of a more general attempt to identify these distinctive methods by talking of philosophy as a second-order activity. This key notion is associated with a number of equally important subsidiary doctrines. It is associated with the view that philosophical tasks are in some way insulated from ground-floor affairs. Even more importantly it is associated with the view that philosophy is primarily concerned with language and with the analysis of language. Such an account seems usefully to explain not only how philosophers may be concerned with topics belonging also to other disciplines, but also the distinctively linguistic nature of their interest in such topics. For on this view philosophers are concerned with the linguistic and not the factual aspects of the topics shared with other disciplines.

Yet it has been noted, too, that the apparent virtues of such an account are accompanied by certain deficiencies. For one thing its generality conceals significant differences between philosophers in the revolution. Even if all revolutionary philosophers were interested in language, still their interests in it were evidently diverse and even sometimes in conflict. Again, although the distinction between science and philosophy rests on certain plain differences in their respective procedures, there are further questions to be raised about the distinction. It may seem plausible to say that if a question is observational or experimental it cannot belong to philosophy, and is more likely to belong to a science. It is much less plausible actually to *identify* scientific questions in terms of such empirical procedures. Yet it is this part of the doctrine which draws the insulating, exclusive, distinction between the two kinds of discipline. If scientific questions were, for example, allowed to range more widely than this, then it would at least be possible for scientific and philosophical questions to overlap.

Even if these initial claims were accepted, however, there would still remain the problem of identifying the kind of non-scientific, non-empirical question which belongs to philosophy. One proposed solution to this problem, of course, lies in the belief that philosophy is a second-order activity and so essentially linguistic. But there are already at least two grounds for doubting the adequacy of such a solution. It has been suggested already that an enquiry may be second-order without being linguistic. But even if this were accepted it should be seriously doubted whether linguistic enquiries can correctly be regarded as neither scientific nor empirical. Once again the steps in the doctrine appear more plausible than perspicuous.

Over and above these difficulties in such a background account of philosophy there are two general issues that might usefully be mentioned. The first of these is the perennial tendency to find a topic or subject-matter for philosophy, and even to claim that enquiry into the topic is scientific. The second is the recurrent tendency to revert to common sense or ordinary language either as an arbiter in philosophical disputes or as a source for material in the subject. Both tendencies can be found in traditional as well as in modern philosophy. Both seem involved, for example, in Hume's remark '. . . philosophical decisions are nothing but the reflections of common life, methodised and corrected'.[1] Both seem equally involved in Warnock's stated aim of acquiring in philosophy what he calls 'systematic conceptual knowledge' through investigation of ordinary language.[2] And both tendencies have a distinctly paradoxical appearance.

In terms of the historical development of the philosophical revolution it is paradoxical enough that at the beginning philosophy should be sharply separated from science, while at the end with Austin and Warnock it should have acquired its own subject-matter to be pursued in a systematic, and scientific, way. It is still more paradoxical to find revolutionaries, such as Reichenbach,

[1] D. Hume, *An Enquiry concerning Human Understanding*, Section XII, Part III.
[2] Warnock, op. cit., pp. 158–9.

accepting the distinction between science and philosophy and at the same time proclaiming that philosophy has at last become a science.[1] That this tendency is more than just a local phenomenon is suggested by similar paradoxes even in traditional philosophers. One of Kant's supposed achievements in his *Critique of Pure Reason* lay in his raising the problem of marking out the boundary between philosophy and science. Popper, indeed, called this problem of demarcation Kant's problem. Yet Kant's major aim in the critical philosophy was precisely to put philosophy on the 'sure path of a science', and the title of his elementary version of the first Critique might justly be translated 'Prolegomena to any future scientific philosophy'.[2]

In a similar way the other tendency, to advert periodically to common sense, is much more than a recent phenomenon in philosophy. Although the popular view of philosophers represents them as deviating extravagantly and incomprehensibly from common sense, almost all traditional philosophers, even Berkeley, profess to follow it. And this conflict is matched by similar disagreements among philosophers about their relationship with common beliefs or ordinary language. It is not at all hard to find in traditional philosophers an appeal to common sense against the excesses of philosophical speculation. Hume, or Locke, or any of the Scottish common-sense philosophers, provide clear illustrations of this tendency. Equally it is not hard to find in the same area severe criticisms of such an appeal to common beliefs in philosophical issues. Kant's attack on the common-sense philosophers in the *Prolegomena*, and Berkeley's dictum that we should 'speak with the vulgar and think with the learned' are examples of the opposite tendency. In recent times this conflict has formed perhaps the major controversy in the development of the philosophical revolution. Some philosophers have found in common sense, or its ordinary language expression, both a weapon to be used in philosophical arguments and source material for philo-

[1] H. Reichenbach, *The Rise of Scientific Philosophy* (California, 1951). Reichenbach's book was published long after the heyday of logical positivism. But its doctrines are very much those of an earlier period. Here are two quotations to indicate the apparent paradox: 'The philosopher speaks an unscientific language because he attempts to answer questions at a time when the means to a scientific answer are not yet at hand' (p. 25); 'There is a body of philosophical knowledge. Philosophy is scientific in its method' (p. 308).

[2] Kant never clearly states what kind of a science philosophy should be, but he interestingly anticipates some recent developments by suggesting in the *Prolegomena* (Section 39) that it should be something like grammar. In holding such a view he appears, rather improbably, to agree with Russell who in *The Principles of Mathematics* (p. 42) also likens philosophy to grammar.

sophical enquiry. Others, such as Gellner, Russell or Mundle,[1] have passionately denied either that the weapon is effective or that the source material is fruitful. Such strong conflicts at least indicate the need for further examination of these positions.

So brief and selective a survey is useful only as a guide to more detailed scrutiny. All the main points so far located will be examined more closely in later chapters, but not primarily from a historical point of view. Anyone who disagrees with this account of the philosophical revolution, or finds that the doctrines mentioned have never been held by particular philosophers, will find the further details detached from any historical reference. But although all the philosophers mentioned would certainly wish to qualify, perhaps sometimes even deny, views which have been ascribed to them, they have sometimes expressed or implied such views, and have certainly been taken by others to have held them. This provides a reason for discussing the views themselves rather than their attachments to particular philosophers. The aim here is to investigate the nature of philosophical tasks and not to applaud or condemn those who have in recent times contributed to our understanding of them.

It is worth while to make these points for two reasons: first because events in recent philosophy are liable to be distorted by strong loyalties and polemical attitudes, and second because it enables me to clarify the attitude of this book. The argument here is not intended as an attack upon modern philosophy or any particular branch of it. Most of the assumptions in the revolution, and much of the work it has inspired, seem to me to be very valuable. But nobody could expect, even wish, that such assumptions should remain for ever unchallenged, and it cannot but be useful to examine and perhaps amend some of them. It would in any case be quite wrong to give the impression that such critical revision is not already taking place. The beliefs of some philosophers, and still more the practice of others, nowadays often run counter to the background principles of the revolution. But these background ideas are not themselves always brought into the open or much discussed. The aim here is rather to formulate satisfactorily some of the background principles which govern philosophical activity than to criticise particular philosophers for their adherence to unsatisfactory principles. In this way it is hoped that two aims may be achieved. The discussion may be useful as an introduction to recent work in philosophy, and perhaps it may make a contribution to its development.

[1] E. Gellner, *Words and Things* (London, 1959) (with a foreword by Russell); C. W. K. Mundle, *A Critique of Linguistic Philosophy* (Oxford, 1970).

2

PHILOSOPHY AND SCIENCE

It has been suggested already that philosophy has a role quite different from that of the sciences, and that an emphasis on this distinction was part of the revolution in philosophy. In his *Tractatus
Logico-Philosophicus* Wittgenstein expressed this claim with particular
force by referring to the propositions of natural science as 'something that has nothing to do with philosophy' (*Tractatus* 6.53).
Certainly a part of the reason for this division lay in the recognition
that while particular sciences may be located in terms of their
subject-matter, there seems to be no comparable topic with which
philosophy alone deals. Wittgenstein again expressed this view by
arguing that if all possible scientific questions were answered then
there would be no questions left (*Tractatus* 6.52). For if this claim
were true, then there would be no domain of enquiry which could
properly be said to concern philosophy rather than some particular
science. It is as if philosophy and science had long competed for
certain areas of enquiry, but the competition had now finally been
won by science. Of course nobody believes that scientists have
already answered all possible questions, but the suggestion is that it is
to them alone that all legitimate questions belong.

But the point about topics is only a sympton of the motive for
dividing philosophy from science, and in other respects the relationship between the two kinds of discipline is obscure. Even to ask a
general question about the relationship between philosophy and
science seems to imply that there is just one kind of science; or at
least that the sciences form a distinct and homogeneous set of
disciplines with varying subject-matter but the same methods and
standards. Such an assumption is certainly misleading. We are much
less clear than this suggests about which disciplines should count as

sciences, and about the criteria for inclusion in the class. It would be wholly wrong to overlook the plain differences between the mathematical and the natural sciences, and equally short-sighted to expect the social or behavioural sciences to be assimilated without remainder into either of these sub-groups. If even such a general sub-division brings to light evident or suspected differences between sciences, then in separating philosophy from science, or in talking of the relationship between them, it cannot be quite clear what philosophy is being compared with. This vagueness has also a more specific consequence. There is a temptation to use the term 'science' indiscriminately to stand for any legitimate enquiry. But in that case it is worth noting that the view ascribed to Wittgenstein, that all legitimate questions belong to science, would be a tautology. In conjunction with the view that philosophy and science are quite distinct and have nothing to do with one another it would then follow that all philosophical tasks are illegitimate.

Certainly such dimly seen consequences need to be kept in mind in the following discussion. But the vagueness which both fosters and blurs these views can be tactically overcome in at least two ways. Either a particular science can be nominated as a standard for comparison, as Descartes nominated arithmetic and algebra, or else the comparison may be made through some feature present in, though not perhaps restricted to, the sciences. Among Professor Berlin's questions, for example, are 'Did the battle of Waterloo take place in the seventeenth century?' which is regarded as non-philosophical, and 'Did the universe have a beginning in time?' which is regarded as philosophical. What is important in the contrast is that there is some generally accepted procedure for answering the first question but none, apparently, for answering the second. Nothing turns here on whether history, to which the first but not the second question belongs, is to be regarded as a science. Whether it is or not, at least some of its claims share with those of the sciences the property of being answerable by some generally accepted procedure, while, it is claimed, philosophical questions enjoy no such answers.

Another inevitable source of confusion in this issue arises from the different aims which may prompt a comparison between science and philosophy. Such comparisons may be made less in the light of what scientists and philosophers actually do, than in the light of certain preconceptions about the tasks and methods of these dis-ciplines. Claims about their relationship may, for example, reflect a desire to recommend a certain picture of philosophy rather than merely to describe its operations. In the first chapter it was noted that philosophers have made recurrent attempts to claim that their discipline is, or ought to be, scientific. It is not hard to see this as a persisting monument to their wish to introduce more rigour, or more uniformity, or more agreement into their discussions. The particular standards of rigour or uniformity will vary with the comparison. Descartes' mathematical standards were different from Hume's Newtonian standards, and these again were different from Reichenbach's logical standards. But all these philosophers were proposing certain tasks or methods for philosophy in the light of a comparison between it and some established discipline. In this chapter some of the background to such comparisons will be presented by contrasting two such pictures of the relationship between philosophy and science. The first picture is certainly pre-revolutionary, with perhaps one proviso to be made later, and might be called 'Cartesian'. The second is closely linked with the revolution and might be called 'Kantian'.

1. *Two pictures of philosophy and science*
The first of these pictures can be briefly drawn in quotations from H. Sidgwick and J. S. Haldane; but they are only representatives of what was a common, and perhaps the official, view in the immediately pre-revolutionary period. In Haldane's book *The Sciences and Philosophy* (p. 175) it is claimed that

the function of philosophy is to enable us to frame as consistent as possible a working conception not merely of part but of the whole of our experience.

And Sidgwick, in his *Philosophy; Its Scope and Relations* (p. ix), says

While the sciences attend to particular parts of the knowable world, philosophy aims at putting them together into a systematic whole.

And he adds later (pp. 10–11) that philosophy may be called in this sense '*scientia scientiarum*'.

This account presents philosophy as a super-science, in some way coordinating all the particular scientific disciplines into one systematic whole. The picture has at once a certain compelling grandeur and a disarming simplicity. It acknowledges realistically that philosophers are more concerned with very general claims than with particular detailed investigations. It offers, too, the hope of a remedy for philosophy's lack of a subject-matter. For on this story its subject-matter may indifferently be regarded either as the sciences themselves (*scientia scientiarum*), or as covering all the topics of the particular sciences (the whole of our experience). In either case Wittgenstein's apparent pessimism at finding only scientific, and therefore no philosophical, questions to answer is frustrated if only because there is no insulating seal to separate science from philosophy. Strictly the account represents the opposition between science and philosophy as spurious. Departmental sciences deal with particular, detailed enquiries in their own delimited fields. What is needed over and above this set of tasks is the comprehensive, supervisory task of integrating the detailed results into a unified system. But the task of fitting these detailed results from different sciences together cannot itself belong to any one of the departmental sciences. It must be allocated to some more general discipline, whose most convenient name is philosophy. Strictly there is no contrast between philosophy and science, but only between a general and a departmental science.

But the apparent advantages and the apparent simplicity of this picture are quite certainly an illusion. How are we to understand the pursuit of this systematic goal, especially when both Sidgwick and Haldane include in it not only all the departmental sciences, but also such things as moral, political, and religious beliefs? It is difficult enough to understand what could be meant by a systematic account of different sciences, such as mathematics, medicine, and economics; it is even more difficult to see how the *same* system is also to embrace moral, political, and religious beliefs as well. It is, of course, difficult also to understand how anyone could have the detailed and encyclopaedic knowledge of all subjects which this systematisation seems to require. 'Seems to require' because we really do not know from such an account what it does require; the idea of such a system is simply too unclear. It is not, therefore, at all surprising to find on examination that neither Sidgwick nor Haldane make any obvious effort to carry out their monumental programme, but content themselves instead with more detailed discussions of quite particular issues.

This evident divorce between the theory and the practice of such philosophers makes it dubious whether their stated aim is a sensible one for philosophers, or an intelligible means of relating philosophy to science. It could perhaps be argued that Sidgwick and Haldane offered their goal only as a distant one to which their detailed enquiries might eventually contribute. But if this point is made, then it cannot be in these terms that philosophy is to be distinguished from science. If, inevitably, philosophers like Sidgwick and Haldane enquire into particular topics, into parts of our experience, then their tasks are not so far distinct from those of the sciences, which also deal, it is said, with parts of our experience. In addition, however, it is well known that scientists themselves have sometimes aimed to unify different branches of science, and no doubt in more speculative moments have dreamed, as Sidgwick and Haldane have, of a total unified science in which all their various branches of enquiry might be brought together. That such dreams are so far fundamentally unintelligible does not put them beyond the range of scientists. But in that case not only does the practice of philosophers fail to support the story, but the theorising of scientists also runs counter to it.

This picture of philosophy, and especially its description of the subject as *scientia scientiarum*, point clearly to a Cartesian background. For Descartes there was no clear generic difference between scientific and philosophical tasks or questions. It is true that even in one of his earliest works, the *Rules for the Direction of the Mind*, Descartes raised very general questions about methods of establishing truth, which seem nowadays to contain recognisably philosophical problems. But his own proposals about method were themselves drawn from the established sciences of his time, namely arithmetic and geometry. In his famous metaphor in the *Rules* (Rule I) Descartes compares the separate branches of enquiry to dark areas intermittently illuminated by the light of reason. What distinguishes departmental sciences from each other is simply the special subject-matter which each observes; but all of them employ a common set of methods to illuminate those distinct areas of enquiry. If such a metaphor is taken seriously, then it will seem obvious that we should identify and cultivate the light of reason which is common to all enquiries, rather than grope after the particular topics which differentiate them.

Inevitably it is a matter of dispute whether Descartes' proposed new method and discipline should be regarded as philosophy at all. Yet the division he suggests between the detailed concerns of departmental sciences and the supervisory task of a new discipline which comprehends them all is plainly like that which Sidgwick and Haldane use to relate science and philosophy. And, with one qualification, it is open to all the obscurities which were found in their picture. From Descartes we understand, as we do not from his successors, that the comprehensive system to be constructed is to be modelled on mathematics, to be deductive and axiomatic. But such a specification makes it no more intelligible how there could be such a comprehensive system containing all the elements of our knowledge and belief.

What, however, is of importance in the picture, if the incoherence can be minimised, is that in it there is no genuine opposition between scientific and philosophical tasks. Perhaps if Descartes had been forced to spell out the differences between science and philosophy he might have admitted that philosophical questions are more abstract than their scientific counterparts; but this would have been quite compatible with his picture of a continuous band of enquiry ranging from the most detailed observation to the most abstract thought. Certainly, as the metaphor shows, Descartes thought that the more general claims had some advantage in certainty and scope. They cover more ground and with more certainty than particular claims, but it is still the same ground that they cover. For Descartes there is no such distinction as that made in recent philosophy between first- and second-order claims, and consequently no discrete jump from scientific to philosophical tasks.

Interestingly Descartes does draw in the *Rules* (Rule XII) a distinction between two kinds of question, namely those that are 'perfectly understood' and those that are 'imperfectly understood'. But there is no suggestion that the former, with standard procedures for their answers, belong to science while the latter belong to philosophy. Equally there is no suggestion that imperfectly understood questions may be spurious or incapable of being answered. The interest in them is precisely that of finding the hidden methods for their resolution and answer. Imperfectly understood questions are not in principle unintelligible, or strongly incapable of being answered; they are not different in kind from perfectly understood questions but only more difficult to understand and answer. In this way the tasks of philosophy and science are not quite distinct; the former are only a more general extension of the latter.

This picture of philosophy merging imperceptibly into science is in fundamental conflict with the doctrines of the revolution. It was challenged in the eighteenth century by Kant and in the twentieth century by the logical positivists. Kant, indeed, held that philosophy in some way stood above all the sciences, and that it was concerned not with parts of experience but with experience as a whole. So far he may appear firmly in the Cartesian tradition. But unlike Descartes he did not think that philosophy should be modelled on an existing science like mathematics, and he argued that the failure of earlier philosophers such as Descartes to separate scientific from philosophical questions had been a potent source of error. For Kant philosophical questions of a traditional kind often arose out of science, but became at a certain stage not merely more general than, but totally different from, scientific questions. A scientist, for example, may ask questions about the causal factors involved in some physical event, but it is not obviously the same sort of question to ask whether every event without exception has a cause. Or again it is one thing to ask a question about the beginning of a process in the universe, say the melting of glaciers on the earth; it is quite another thing to ask a question about the beginning of the universe itself. Evidently processes in the universe can have their beginnings located by reference to other prior events, but the universe itself, as an entity that encompasses all events, cannot have its beginning located by reference to any prior events. In Kant's terminology questions which in this way seem to take off from ordinary experience and yet seem to stand no chance of an answer in terms of that experience are called 'transcendent'. To such questions, he claimed, to say 'There is no answer' is itself the only answer we can give.

With this step Kant finally abandoned any belief in the Cartesian picture. For Descartes some questions may be more general than others or more difficult to answer, and the former may belong typically to philosophy rather than to any departmental science, but there is no hint that philosophical questions may be quite unanswerable. Kant's recognition that we may, even are bound to, raise questions in philosophy to which in principle there can be no answer begins to draw a quite new kind of contrast between science and philosophy. Kant did not speak of science as a first-order activity or of philosophy as second-order; nor did he speak of science as factual and of philosophy as linguistic or conceptual. But when he noted the existence of a class of typically philosophical questions which were in principle unanswerable, and about which controversy and disagreement were equally futile, he anticipated the revolutionary view that science and philosophy are separate kinds of discipline. Questions such as these are imperfectly understood in a way which was not recognised in the Cartesian picture. It might indeed be said that such questions are not just imperfectly understood so much as perfectly unintelligible. If this category of question is acknowledged to exist and is used to mark a division between philosophy and science, then the Cartesian picture is decisively rejected. In place of a continuity between the particular enquiries of departmental science and the general questions of philosophy, which allows a smooth transition from one to the other, there then exists a sharp line of demarcation, a frontier post, between the disciplines. As a matter of history, after Kant the frontier was difficult to cross, if not actually closed.

One clear reason for this, at least in the twentieth century, is that the Kantian picture unlike the Cartesian is certainly revolutionary, both in its sharp division between philosophy and science and in its emphasis on a special kind of mistake to which philosophers are prone. There are, as we shall see, other respects in which some revolutionary philosophers, particularly logical positivists, still retained some links with the Cartesian doctrines. But in these two respects they, and most other revolutionaries, sided with Kant. Kant certainly had a different label for the erroneous questions; he would have called them 'transcendent' rather than simply meaningless. But both Kant and the positivists would have agreed that the central mistake arose from a fundamental confusion about the kind of question that previous philosophers had asked. In Waismann's book *The Principles of Linguistic Philosophy* a remedial attention to the nature of these questions, instead of a simple Cartesian desire to answer them, is regarded as a major principle in the revolution. He says (p. 4)

The great mistake of philosophers up to now, which has led to so many misunderstandings, is that they have produced answers before seeing clearly the nature of the questions they have been asking. They seem to have been unaware of the possibility that the form of the question itself might conceal an error.

Such a remark would not be out of place in the Dialectic of Kant's *Critique of Pure Reason*.

2. *Lines of demarcation*
The Cartesian picture strictly draws no sharp line of demarcation between science and philosophy. By contrast the Kantian picture at least indicates one such frontier, in which to move from science to philosophy is to move from answerable questions to those which are in various ways confused, empty, and unanswerable. Since it is the latter rather than the former picture which appealed to philosophers in the revolution it is important to consider briefly some of its apparent consequences. It hardly needs to be said how much this Kantian picture supports an exclusive distinction between philosophy and science of the kind drawn by Wittgenstein, Berlin, and Peters. If philosophical questions are typically unanswerable, either meaningless or transcendent, then it is entirely natural to contrast them with the legitimate and answerable questions belonging to science.

One consequence of such a view is that there may then seem to be no room for philosophical questions, and no scope therefore for philosophical tasks. If it is held that philosophical questions are in principle unanswerable, so that any proferred answers to them cannot be separated as good or bad, well or badly grounded, then it appears that they cannot have any genuine function. They reflect only a certain pathology of the intellect in which, for example, one may persistently search for the beginning of the universe as though the task were just like locating the beginning of an epidemic. To adopt this principle of demarcation makes it certain that such traditional questions and the tasks associated with giving answers to them are simply spurious. It encourages the *Tractatus* view that all legitimate questions belong to science.

To conclude from this that there are no genuine tasks in philosophy would be nevertheless premature. During the revolution at least three ways of reinstating such tasks were tried. In the first of these the task of philosophers was not to raise, still less attempt to answer, the confused traditional questions, but instead to elucidate the mistakes which prompted them. It was in terms of this activitiy of removing the puzzlement at the root of such questions that philosophy came to be thought of as therapeutic. In theory when the original question had been clarified the desire for an answer to it had also been removed. Kant certainly held a similar view of the questions he regarded as transcendent. Although there was no direct answer to be given to them, at least it could be shown why this was so. But Kant was less optimistic about the power of such a therapy, for he regarded these questions as arising so inevitably from our own situation that they could never finally be dismissed.

This account of philosophy as therapeutic may seem to add weight to another revolutionary doctrine, namely the idea that philosophy is a second-order activity. For if instead of raising and answering the traditional questions philosophers turn to the activity of scrutinising the questions themselves, then their activity certainly seems to have moved to a new level. Where before there were merely questions and rival answers to them, now there are preliminary questions to be raised about the original questions themselves. Certainly on this account philosophy has moved a step back to undertake a preliminary reconnaissance, but this does not strictly justify the whole doctrine of second-order activities. For one thing, if the original questions were themselves of a higher order than those of the sciences, philosophy is actually represented as at least a third-order activity. More seriously this argument is clearly different from those in which philosophy's higher order is due to its interest in the sciences, or to its specifically linguistic interests. There is no general reason, for example, to suppose that any preliminary difficulty raised about an enquiry must be linguistic in nature. If this should seem so, then it may be because we describe this activity as that of scrutinising questions, and confusedly think of questions, as opposed to enquiries, as specifically linguistic phenomena.

A second move that might be made to retain some function for philosophy depended upon the location of a class of legitimate questions which were nevertheless not empirical. For if there were a class of such questions, and if philosophical questions were included in the class, then there would be room for philosophical tasks outside the area of empirical scientific enquiry. And there is a typical class of such non-empirical questions in such disciplines as mathematics and formal logic. The logical positivist classification of meaningful statements into those which are empirically verifiable and those which are necessarily true was an acknowledgment of this area of non-empirical enquiry. In such a context while there is no reference to empirical observation there are procedures for deciding on the answers to its questions. Hence it is possible to account for the function of philosophical claims which are non-empirical and yet decidable and meaningful, by locating them within the area of formal logic. The existence and development in the revolution of the apparatus of modern logic undoubtedly gave a special impetus to this move, in which philosophy came to be thought of primarily as pure or applied formal logic. It is hardly necessary to stress how much this view encourages the idea that philosophy is a second-order, linguistic, and analytic activity.

This second move is not incompatible with the first account of therapeutic clarification, but it certainly faces in another direction. One way of achieving a certain standard of clarity would be to reformulate obscure claims in the lucid notation of formal logic, but certainly Wittgenstein's therapeutic practice rarely used formal logic and in some respects even implied a rejection of the technique. Moreover the logical positivists who played this second move exploited it not in order to separate philosophy from science but in order to bring it to bear upon the existing sciences. For them the central positive task of philosophy lay in the 'rational reconstruction' of the sciences, and was not restricted merely to a piecemeal therapy. Rational reconstruction certainly involved the reformulation of scientific claims, and of whole theories, in terms of the apparatus of modern logic. It was precisely this novel ability to carry out such a programme which led to the claim, made for example by Reichenbach, that philosophy had at last become scientific.

B

Such a development is plainly in conflict with Wittgenstein's view in the *Tractatus* that philosophy has nothing to do with the propositions of natural science. It is also one important way in which the pre-revolutionary Cartesian picture and the revolutionary view seem to share common ground. For the programme of rational reconstruction is Cartesian in spirit. Philosophy appears in it as a supervisory discipline reformulating and even regulating the claims of departmental science. It is, consequently, not so surprising to find that the logical positivists were also dedicated to the further Cartesian idea of a unified science. Philosophy in this style not only reformulated scientific theories in the perspicuous terms of modern logic, but also aimed to bring about a unification of different branches of science within these logical systems. Positivists could perhaps still not have accepted the Cartesian idea of a smooth transition from philosophy to science. For their programme was essentially one of translation and rearrangement in a technical language. Their activities were linguistic, analytic, and second-order and so differed in kind from the substantive first-order enquiries of the scientists whose work they reconstructed.

It is finally not hard to see in this background one further development in the revolution. If philosophy is to be quite unrelated to science and concerned with language, then nothing could be more natural than that philosophical tasks should come to be directed towards the non-technical concepts of ordinary life. No doubt this provided one motive for the philosophical interest in ordinary language, but in other respects this development appears less straightforward. One supporting ground for such a move might be, for example, the belief that many issues in philosophy, such as scepticism, did not concern any particular science and could even arise independently of any science. It is easy to see that the same kind of doubt about other people's emotional states or their genuine, as opposed to expressed, attitudes and beliefs can arise just as much in everyday contexts as in the technical areas of psychiatry or psychology. But although such a motive pushes the direction of philosophical interest away from technical and towards ordinary language, it has also the counter-revolutionary tendency to focus attention on traditional issues such as scepticism. It is true that the attention mainly took the form of devising new therapies to cure the old confusions, but the multiplication of such cures suggested that even traditional issues were not so easily dismissed.

In the light of this tendency it is again entirely natural that philosophers should have found the consultant role of therapeutic philosophy somewhat restrictive. Ordinary people are less willing to note and less anxious to treat their intellectual than their physical ills. Philosophical therapy tended therefore to concentrate on the special maladies of philosophers themselves. It is a testimony to the restricting nature of such a task that philosophers like Austin and Warnock should seek a more systematic account of the concepts of ordinary language. Such an aim might still be therapeutic, but designed to discover and prevent new confusions rather than to continue curing the old ones. Warnock's aim of acquiring in philosophy what he called 'systematic conceptual knowledge' is a natural extension of this programme (see p. 21). It has the triple appeal of providing a systematic rather than a haphazard task, of avoiding well-worn traditional issues, and of finding a subject-matter for philosophy which is in some way excluded from any branch of science. It is this subject-matter to which Peters referred when he spoke of the 'clarification of meaning' as a philosophical task to be excluded from the empirical enquiries of scientists (see p. 14).

3. An assessment

Each of the manœuvres plotted in the previous section depends upon an exclusive distinction of kind between philosophy and science. One way of being driven to one or other of these positions involves the acceptance of such a fundamental separation between the disciplines. For if there were no such exclusive contrast to be drawn, then philosophical tasks would not have to be merely therapeutic, or wholly non-empirical, or directed only to ordinary language. Of course such views as these might still give a correct account of some philosophical tasks even if the background separation were wholly mistaken. It will not be questioned here that philosophers may contribute to the clarification of confused ideas, or that they may use the apparatus of formal logic to reformulate scientific theories, or that they may study systematically the features of ordinary language. Nevertheless if the background distinction were unjustified it would at least not be necessary to adopt any of these positions, in order to find legitimate tasks for philosophy. In that case it would not be necessary to restrict philosophical tasks to these areas; it would be possible to think of philosophical and scientific tasks as overlapping rather than separate.

The argument of this section is designed to show that the quoted representatives of this background view are unjustified, so that the subsequent manœuvres are unnecessary. But the background view is certainly complex. Berlin's claims are not exactly the same as those of Peters, and Peters' claims may not have quite the same force as those of Wittgenstein. As we have already seen Berlin is not explicitly contrasting philosophy and science, in the way that both Peters and Wittgenstein are. Nevertheless it is natural to treat Berlin's distinction between questions for which there are, and others for which there are not, expert answers as only a more general account of the distinction between philosophy and science. I shall examine the claims made by Berlin and Peters and then draw some general conclusions from the discussion in the light of the two pictures, the Cartesian and the Kantian, with which the chapter began.

So far Berlin's illustrative questions have been only sampled, and it is helpful to have the whole list.

Philosophical questions	*Non-philosophical questions*
Are there any material objects in the universe (or does it perhaps consist rather of minds and their states)?	Have any ravens been seen in Iceland in 1955?
Did the universe have a beginning in time?	Did the battle of Waterloo take place in the seventeenth century?
Can I ever be quite certain about what goes on in the mind of another?	Are you quite certain that he knows you?
Why are the predictions of scientists more reliable than those of witch-doctors?	Why is Einstein's theory superior to Newton's?
Are there irrational numbers?	How many positive roots are there to the equation $x^2 = 2$?
What is the exact meaning of the word 'if'?	What is the exact meaning of the word 'obscurantist'?
How should I (or men in general) live?	How should I mend this broken typewriter?

Of the philosophical questions Berlin says that they 'tend to be very general, to involve issues of principle, and to have little or no concern with practical utility'. These features could not of course generally mark out philosophical from scientific questions, since many of the latter will certainly be very general, involve issues of principle and have little or no concern with practical utility. But even among Berlin's examples such a contrast is at least not obvious. The question 'Why is Einstein's theory superior to Newton's?' might be said to have these typically philosophical features, while, if we attach a sense to the term 'material object' which allows tables and chairs to be material objects, to ask if there are any material objects in the universe might seem to have considerable practical interest.

It is also in general puzzling that often the non-philosophical question appears to be only a particular instance of the corresponding philosophical question. If I am quite certain that Jones knows me, and if knowing someone at least involves something that 'goes on in the mind', then this seems to provide an answer also to the corresponding philosophical question. Equally if the answer to the latter question is 'No', then the answer to the former must also be negative, if we make the same assumptions. Such relationships between the philosophical and non-philosophical questions preserve the contrast between the former's generality and the latter's particularity, but they make it incomprehensible how the former can have little or no concern with practical utility, while this is not true of the latter.

These distinguishing features as tendencies cannot perhaps be expected to distinguish decisively between individual questions. It is not surprising therefore that Berlin should appeal to the criterion that has been so far stressed as 'even more characteristic' of philosophical questions, namely that 'there seem to be no obvious and generally accepted procedures for answering them, nor any class of specialists to whom we automatically turn for their solutions'. But even here it is not at all easy to discern this distinction in the offered illustrations. If, for example, the above-noted relationship of general to particular question does hold between any pair of contrasted questions, then there will be an obvious and widely accepted procedure for answering the philosophical question precisely in terms of an answer to the corresponding non-philosophical question. The procedure which enables me to say that I am certain that Jones knows me will, on the given assumptions, also enable me to be certain of what goes on in the mind of another.

Again it would be quite natural to expect a specialist in mathematics to answer the question about the existence of irrational numbers, while it may seem doubtful whether there are experts who might provide a direct answer to the question 'Why is Einstein's theory superior to Newton's?' This last question presumably depends for its answer on the criteria for superiority among scientific theories, but it is by no means obvious what these criteria should be, or which experts might tell us what they are. As a question about science rather than within any particular science there is some reason for allocating the question not to any scientist but to someone who has surveyed generally the different types of scientific theory. Certainly in the Cartesian story such a man would be called a philosopher, and philosophers have indeed concerned themselves with this question.

Similarly the question 'Did the universe have a beginning in time?', although classed as a philosophical question, has been asked and answered by physicists interested in cosmology. And finally the question 'What is the exact meaning of the word "if"?' hardly seems to differ significantly from its non-philosophical counterpart. Both questions seem to concern lexicographers who presumably have some agreed procedures for answering their questions about the meanings of words. Certainly the word 'if' is of special interest to logicians, and this provides some reason for allocating the question to philosophy. But in that case we should have to admit that the philosophical questions may also belong to other disciplines; and in general that the two categories of philosophical and non-philosophical questions do not exclude each other. It is not difficult to find in other cases the same failure of exclusiveness, and a consequent overlap, between the two kinds of question.

It would be wrong to believe that nothing can be gained from a consideration of Berlin's contrasted questions. The immediate conclusion to be drawn is only that their demonstration value is limited; they do not by themselves reveal the claimed distinctions. If in the end their allocation to different disciplines were to be agreed, then this would be because something had been independently learned of the contrast between science and philosophy, and not because of their own illuminative power. It is tempting, for example, to say that a school pupil's question 'Are there irrational numbers?' might reasonably be answered by the mathematics teacher, but that this is not the question listed as philosophical. No doubt philosophers know the answer to that question and are interested in asking a different question of a more subtle kind. A similar point was made earlier about the existence of material objects in the universe. But in that case the list of questions needs to be supplemented by additional information about the difference between a philosophical and a non-philosophical question when they are expressed in exactly the same words.

Influenced perhaps by the difficulties of drawing clear and decisive distinctions in these terms Berlin goes on to make Reichenbach's point that at least many philosophical problems arise just when scientists ask questions which they have not yet the resources or techniques to answer. Berlin speaks of the clarification of problems in the sciences which nevertheless leaves behind

a nucleus of unresolved (and largely unanalysed) questions whose generality, obscurity, and, above all, apparent (or real) insolubility by empirical or formal methods gives them a status of their own which we tend to call philosophical.[1]

Such an account offers the hope of a more satisfactory understanding of the contrasts between the pairs of questions, and of the contrast between philosophical and scientific questions. It suggests that these contrasts are not after all exclusive, and that it is only natural to find, as we did, that philosophical and non-philosophical questions may overlap. Although at the beginning Berlin's account appeared to be Kantian and revolutionary, at the end it has taken a decidedly Cartesian turn.

It would be natural to say in the light of the criticisms of Berlin's examples that they do not by themselves show the general contrast to be mistaken. Even if it were admitted that Berlin's illustrative cases are inadequate in revealing an exclusive distinction between science and philosophy, still the general distinction might be correct. The quotation from Peters, however, is a quite general expression of such a distinction, and offers no particular examples at all. It presents a contrast between the scientists' empirical questions and the philosophers' questions about meaning or language in a way which reflects typically some of the revolutionary ideas which have been so far mentioned. In particular, it distinguishes philosophical enquiries from those of science by means of an exclusive contrast of level between questions of fact and questions of language. Not only is philosophy quite separate from science, but the barrier between them shows that they involve different levels of activity. But in order to justify this separation two assumptions have to be made which are at best very dubious. It has to be assumed first that scientific questions are simply empirical in character; and second that enquiry into meaning or language is neither empirical nor scientific.

Of the first assumption it is hard to say anything other than that it is plainly false. Certainly it would be wrong to *identify* scientific with empirical questions, if only because there are plenty of empirical questions ('Did I lock the front door?') which are not scientific. But it would be equally short-sighted to make the identification in the face of disciplines such as mathematics, which may be regarded as sciences but whose questions are not empirical. Hence it is natural

[1] Berlin, op. cit., p. 13.

to construe the claim as a one-way entailment between natural science and empirical enquiry. Perhaps not all empirical questions belong to some science, and perhaps some sciences are not empirical, but at least it may seem correct to claim that if a question belongs to a natural science, then it is empirical.

It can indeed scarcely be denied that there is a strong connection between natural science and the procedures of experiment and empirical test, but this falls short of establishing that all scientific enquiries are empirical. If the standard empirical enquiry consists in applying a set of established principles to some so far untested phenomenon, then it is clear that not all scientific enquiries are of this sort. Such enquiries belong to the routine of what Kuhn has called 'normal' science.[1] To suppose that such work exhausts the range of scientific activity is to give a quite one-sided view of such disciplines. It is to suggest that science demands no more than the virtues of industry in applying unquestioned principles to new areas. But just as it cannot be denied that much science is of this kind so it cannot be denied that scientists sometimes not only apply established techniques, but also develop new ones, not only work within accepted principles, but also devise new principles. In Kuhn's terminology science may be revolutionary as well as normal. If applying accepted principles to untested phenomena is the standard empirical enquiry, then questioning old and formulating new principles is an enquiry of a quite different kind.

Again there is a difference between an empirical claim in applied engineering, such as 'This bridge will collapse if a 200-ton weight is moved across it', and a claim in pure physics, such as Newton's first law, 'Every body perseveres in its state of rest or of uniform motion in a straight line, except in so far as it is compelled to change that state by forces impressed on it'. Such a difference appears to engage the contrast between empirical and non-empirical claims, but it is not easy to evaluate when it is not clear exactly what the term 'empirical' is being contrasted with. But when the contrast is, as in Peters' quotation, between empirical questions and questions about meaning, then it must seem wholly wrong to exclude the latter from the domain of science. For there can be no doubt that scientists raise and answer questions about the meanings of their terms, just as they also raise and answer questions of the contrasted empirical kind. Indeed it has often been thought that at least sometimes when scientists devise new principles they are precisely raising and answering questions about the meanings of their terms. Einstein's

[1] T. S. Kuhn, *The Structure of Scientific Revolutions* (Chicago, 1966).

account of the term 'simultaneity' and the eighteenth-century debate about the term 'momentum' provide prima facie examples of this kind of scientific activity.[1] In such cases the activity might be described in terms of a search for, and possibly a change in, the criteria for the application of a term. Perhaps it is characteristic of the feeblest kind of normal science that the criteria for its terms should be simply accepted and applied without question. But in other contexts it can scarcely be imagined that scientists are quite unconcerned about the meanings of their terms.

Nor is the second assumption, that enquiry into meaning is neither empirical nor scientific, any more plausible than the first. It is true that in the scientific cases just mentioned an enquiry into the meaning of a term will naturally be contrasted with a standard empirical enquiry. Certainly it will look and feel different from a standard empirical enquiry to the scientists engaged in it. And this may encourage the view that all enquiries into meaning are non-empirical. But there are two strong objections to such an inference. In the first place, although it is natural to contrast these activities, it may still be misleading to describe the revision of criteria as non-empirical. Such revisions would be expected to have empirical consequences, and even in a roundabout way to be testable by reference to facts about the success or failure of the theory of which they form a dominant part.

In the second place, however, it would also be wrong to extend this account of an enquiry into meaning to cover all such enquiries. Linguists, philologists, and even grammarians investigate language and meaning in a way which seems intuitively quite different from the scientists' worries about criteria. Linguistic studies of these kinds are certainly often empirical, and are often regarded also as scientific. It is true that at present the study of meaning in natural languages has been less successful than some other branches of linguistic enquiry, but to imagine that it could never achieve the status of an established science requires an act of faith of a quite arbitrary kind. The existence and prospects of such studies provide evidence for the simple falsity of the second assumption. Later (in Chapter 4) we shall find that revolutionary philosophers sometimes appealed to a supposedly non-empirical semantics in order to define their own special tasks. But this appeal is so doubtful, and the belief in it so surrounded by confusions, that it would not make sense here simply to assume its authenticity. At this stage, then, neither of the assump-

[1] See, for example, F. Waismann, *The Principles of Linguistic Philosophy*, Ed. R. Harré (London, 1965), ch. 1.

tions required by Peters' view to establish an exclusive division between science and philosophy can be accepted.

The number of mistakes and ambiguities in the quoted accounts suggests that the doctrine behind them had become too deeply embedded in the revolution to be seriously scrutinised. Yet it would be surprising if there were not some elementary truth behind the doctrine which made the latter appear unquestionable. And it is not too difficult to find in these views a basic truth whose distortion is responsible for these mistakes. For in all of them there is an implicit contrast between simply answering clear questions, of whose answers we are ignorant, and clarifying, or analysing, or resolving complexities in questions which are in some way obscure. It can scarcely be doubted that both activities are valuable, even necessary, in any serious investigation. The contrast, in particular, is not confined merely to empirical questions, but covers also the questions which might arise in mathematics or logic. But, of course, just for that reason it would be quite wrong to hold that one of these activities, clarification, is exclusively the concern of philosophy, and the other, providing answers, is exclusively the concern of science. To take such a view would be to characterise science as always normal and philosophy as always revolutionary, in Kuhn's senses of these terms. It would be, quite unplausibly, to deny that science was ever revolutionary or philosophy ever normal. Yet some questions in science are undoubtedly revolutionary, and some enquiries in philosophy are undoubtedly normal. It may be that philosophy is more often revolutionary and science more often normal, but even if there is such a ground for associating one kind of activity more closely with one kind of discipline still it cannot be to draw an exclusive distinction between these disciplines. It seems that only a powerful dogma could prevent us from admitting that both kinds of activity are pursued in both science and philosophy.

The basic truth behind the revolutionary picture cannot therefore support that picture in drawing any exclusive contrast between the tasks of philosophy and science. On the contrary it rather supports the alternative view that there must be some common ground or overlap between these tasks. Some scientific activities may also deserve the epithet 'philosophical', and some philosophers' tasks may deserve the description 'scientific'. To hold such a view is to accept the Cartesian picture at least in a weak form purified of its incoherence. It is therefore not surprising that the basic truth identified in the distorted revolutionary doctrine amounts to the Cartesian division between perfectly and imperfectly understood questions. Descartes did not make the further claim that to disentangle the latter questions was always a matter of language and not of fact. He thus avoided both some of the insights and some of the mistakes of his revolutionary successors. But it is interesting again to see how the revolutionary doctrine, although apparently opposed to the Cartesian picture, in the end seems to resolve into it. At least one philosopher in the revolution explicitly drew these Cartesian conclusions, though they were not echoed by the philosophers I have quoted. In his *The Principles of Linguistic Philosophy* Waismann made his own Cartesian position plain when he wrote

If laying bare the structure of concepts, the analysis of language, the clarification of meaning is the peculiar task of the philosopher, then we must say that the philosophical attitude is an essential part of all scientific thought.[1]

---

[1] Waismann, op. cit., p. 14. See also M. Schlick, 'The Future of Philosophy' in R. Rorty (Ed.), *The Linguistic Turn* (Chicago, 1967), pp. 49, 52–3.

3

PHILOSOPHY AND HISTORY

So far philosophical tasks, and especially the features which distinguish them from scientific enquiries, have been considered quite
generally. Few philosophical questions have been identified, and
none has been even tentatively answered. Even where such questions
have been noted, as in Berlin's list, they were found to be described
in an unilluminating way. Now it is time to look in more detail at a
particular philosophical problem, not so much for its own sake but
rather to illustrate something of the structure which such problems
have. With suitable qualifications we may hope to draw some
morals about philosophical tasks even from this one case. And
since the problem to be discussed is about another discipline, namely
history, it is reasonable to hope that the discussion may reveal
something of the relationship that holds between philosophy and
other disciplines. The question is simply whether history should be
regarded as a subjective or an objective study.[1]

It would certainly be wrong to regard this question as exactly
like all other philosophical questions, and even premature to treat
it as typical of them. But one assumption which will not be questioned
here is that the issue really is philosophical. Indeed it is partly
because of this assumption that historians themselves have tended
to shy away from the issue, as though it were of only limited interest
beside their own detailed enquiries into the past. Yet few historians
would want entirely to reject the question as of no concern to them,
and they have even evolved a stock response to it. If they are asked
whether history is subjective they are likely to say such things as:

---

[1] The discussion here is inevitably limited and schematic. A lengthier treatment
with added references may be found in W. H. Walsh, *An Introduction to Philosophy
of History* (London, 1951), chs. 3, 4 and 5.

I always say at the beginning of my lecture course that I am biassed, and that what I say inevitably reflects my own personal views. And this, I think, makes it clear to the students where they stand.

Or again:

I don't think a historian can ever be completely objective. He can, and ought to, try to overcome his prejudices and bias, but there will always be a residual subjectivity in his work.[1]

The stock response acknowledges usefully some of the key terms in the issue, for example those of 'bias', 'prejudice', and 'complete objectivity'. It has also the consequence, which a historian may welcome, of blocking further discussion by at once conceding a certain subjectivity, without greatly straining the professional conscience. For these answers depict the historian as a reluctant but honest victim of an inevitable handicap. Once the concession is made there seems no room for further discussion. The stock response functions like a plea of guilty but insane, or like an honest admission of guilt coupled with a plea for mercy. There is no longer need to discuss the verdict, but only to consider leniently the sentence.

But however effective such answers have been in stopping further discussion, there is good reason not to be satisfied with them. Whether in the end they are right or wrong, they accept at face value the dichotomy, between subjective and objective, in terms of which the question is put; and it is by no means clear that it should be so readily accepted. What, after all, is the distinction between what is subjective and what is objective? By what standards, precisely, is history being judged? What is it exactly that historians miss in failing to be 'completely objective'? And how do historians, unlike chemists or biologists or doctors, come to be residually tainted in this way? These are questions which need to be answered before the stock response itself can be either accepted or rejected. It is an uncontroversial part of the task of philosophers to tease such answers out.

[1] These are fictional conflations of views that are nevertheless often held. In a recent *Scotsman* report of an address at a graduation ceremony (6 July 1968) a professor of history is alleged to have made the following points. (1) Arts subjects are more fun than science subjects. 'They are more fun because they are so evidently the product of human trial and error, so inescapably subjective.' (2) The scientist is also looking at situations of which he forms a part. 'But he pretends he isn't, and the Arts man doesn't. We are rich in our doubts. We know we can never be right. How can you be right about Virgil, or Shakespeare, or James VI and I? How can you be right about anything that is the creation and the creature of the human predicament?' These remarks fall solidly within the tradition of the stock response.

Perhaps one of the historian's motives for evading these further questions arises from the idea that since they, like the original question, belong to philosophy, they have no bearing on historical enquiry. This is the reverse side of the same coin in which philosophers are apt to represent their enquiries as quite insulated from other disciplines. Another motive may be a certain modesty with which historians generally approach the question whether their discipline ranks as a science. To admit even a residual subjectivity might appear damaging to a claim to be a science, but if historians are not anxious to make such a claim for their subject then a certain lack of objectivity will be more acceptable. It is worth noting that the background is quite different in another context where the same basic issue has arisen. Sociologists, unlike historians, have wanted to regard their discipline as a science. Their contributions to the enquiry as to whether a social science is possible show that the issue in that context is not merely academic. It is worth remembering this wider context, but for our purposes it is better to raise the question in relation to history, where the issue is less urgent.

What has so far been said suggests the two main lines of argument to be pursued here. In the first of these an attempt is made to isolate the features which history lacks in failing to be objective. In this variation the answer to the original question depends upon a comparison of history with established natural sciences. It is assumed that these sciences are themselves objective, and therefore that any discipline which is subjective must differ significantly from them. What, in this line, historians lack when they fail to attain complete objectivity is some standard of achievement present in, even set by, the natural sciences.

In the second variation the emphasis is placed less on the study of history itself than on the historian. For in the stock response it is the historian who succumbs to a residual subjectivity. It is he who, in the end, cannot keep his personal views, his bias and prejudice, out of the enquiries he undertakes. While the first line of argument measures the study of history against standards set by other objective disciplines, the second line points to distorting factors present in the historian. It would be wrong to expect that the two variations are quite separate from each other; we shall find several points at which they overlap. It would also be wrong to expect the discussion to be at all comprehensive. What is important here is the general structure of the main variations rather than the detailed pursuit of all the branching lines within them.

Variation 1. History and natural science

Plainly there are a number of differences between the disciplines we now know as history and the natural sciences. For one thing exact measurement is fundamental in the latter but not in the former. This is not to say that measurement is of no importance in history, or that mathematics has no application to the data of history. But the role of measurement and the application of statistical methods in history are certainly less extensive and less important than they are in the natural sciences. Again controlled laboratory experiment is an essential technique in these sciences, but it plays almost no part in historical enquiry at all. Finally the subject-matter of the two kinds of discipline is significantly different. History is concerned less with inanimate objects than with people, their activities and institutions. Even where the natural sciences deal with people, as in medicine, persistent reminders are in order that patients are human and not inanimate objects, as though science imposes a tendency to dehumanise its objects. In all these obvious ways historians grapple with a more recalcitrant, less measurable, and less controllable set of data than is to be found in the sciences. Such differences do not show that science is, while history is not, objective but they point to other relevant contrasts between the two kinds of enquiry.

Nothing has so far been said of the most obvious feature of historical enquiry, namely that it deals with the past. Of course it is true that natural sciences are also inevitably interested in what has already happened, but they are not restricted to such an interest in the way that history is. Scientists, like historians, derive their data from the past; indeed all data are necessarily historical. But that the scientists' direction of interest is importantly away from the past appears in two closely related ways. First it appears in the attempt to formulate quite general laws governing the data, and second in the use of such laws to predict what will happen in the future. For a scientist the more general the explanatory theory the more fundamental it is felt to be, and the more valuable as a predictive device. But in history enquiry is more obviously directed towards particular events in the past, rather than to the formulation of general laws or predictions. We might say that the scientist's data are inevitably restricted to the past but that his conclusions are not; while for the historian both data and conclusions are restricted to the past. It is not an accident that many historians express distaste for the glib phrase 'History shows us that . . .'. It is true that historians do not merely narrate what has happened; such a view of the subject would be very naive. But although they provide some explanation of past events there are reasons for saying that such explanation does not fit those events into a framework of specifically historical laws.

Certainly historians are as a matter of fact more interested in examining a particular economy in the nineteenth century than in providing a general theory about the development of any capitalist economy. But more than that, anyone who claimed to provide such a theory might naturally be regarded less as a historian than as an economist. It would be easy, and wrong, to exaggerate the sharpness of such a division. Undoubtedly history interacts with economics and with sociology and indeed with almost every other explanatory discipline. But the fact that historians are generally more concerned with particular events is only another aspect of the tendency to regard any general laws used by historians as economic, or social, or political laws rather than as specifically historical principles. Indeed it might be said that the idea of a law of history is as absurd as that of a law of development. There are no laws of development as such, but only laws governing the development of this or that entity.

Some philosophers and historians may wish to dispute these points. In a recent book,[1] for example, Professor Körner rightly criticises those who argue that historical explanations are never like those in the natural sciences. He argues that it is perfectly possible, even common, for a historian to explain such an event as Napoleon's order to retreat from Moscow by using a schema such as:

Napoleon was in a situation with such and such features. Everybody in such a situation gives the order to retreat. Therefore Napoleon gave the order to retreat.

Although the explanation has a certain formal baldness there is no doubt that similar accounts may be found in history books. But Körner also suggests that the illustration shows the existence of general laws of history in a way which may appear to deny what I have claimed. That the illustration does not count against this view can be seen by considering the status of the only general proposition in the schema. Such a claim as 'Everybody in such a situation gives the order to retreat' is presumably either a principle of military science, or a related rule of common-sense psychology. Neither interpretation indicates any specifically historical law. The illustration even suggests that historians do, or must, borrow their explana-

[1] S. Körner, *Fundamental Questions in Philosophy* (London, 1971), pp. 153-5.

tory laws either from other disciplines or from common sense. It would be premature to claim that there are no other kinds of explanation in history, but the existence of these borrowed forms suggests an important difference between history and the natural sciences. The phenomenon might be described as an explanatory gap in history, which both measures its deviation from science and also provides a possible location for its lack of objectivity.

This so-called explanatory gap is related to the historian's interest in *particular* events in the past in contrast to the scientist's concern with open classes of event. But there is another kind of gap in history which arises from the historian's interest in particular events in the *past*. It may seem natural, for this reason, that the historian cannot exercise the kind of control over his data which the scientist normally expects in his laboratory experiments. Many events in the past are so well attested that they may never be doubted; others that we are now ignorant of may be unearthed later; and others may remain for ever undisclosed. It is not generally open to a historian, as it may seem to be to a scientist, to discover evidence almost at will through the application of an experimental test. It is not hard to add such a factual gap to the gap in explanation, and allow both to give force to the view that historians create as much history as they discover. No doubt that would be a misleading exaggeration. It would be more plausible to see in these gaps some basis for the claimed subjectivity of history.

These points provide in this variation the basic data for a conclusion about history's residual subjectivity. What remains to be done is to assess the force of such arguments; and here the first move must be to question the relevance of any of the cited points. What has been shown is that there are important differences between history and the natural sciences. But it certainly does not follow from the fact that a discipline differs from natural science that it is not objective. Even if it were granted that for these reasons history is not a natural science, it would still not follow that history is not objective. If this conclusion were thought to follow it would be because it was assumed that the terms 'objective' and 'scientific' have the same meaning, or at least that the second property is a logical consequence of the first. But as an unreflective assumption either of these beliefs would be a mistake, as clear as the choice of a move in chess which leads unavoidably to defeat. Anyone who is prepared to infer the subjectivity of history directly from the data so far presented can be simply refuted in this way. The position is untenable because accepting that the sciences are objective, and even that they are paradigm instances of an objective discipline, does not mean that to be scientific and to be objective are the same thing. It is, of course, natural that the paradigm instances of objectivity at any time should come to be identified with the property itself, just as it was natural for Descartes in the seventeenth century to take the established sciences of his time as a model for other disciplines. But Descartes' procedure has generally been regarded as a disastrous mistake, and the temptation to treat any difference from natural science as demonstrating subjectivity is no less of an error.

This does not mean, however, that the whole strategy of the present variation is unsound. It does show that if the accepted differences between history and natural science are to be relevant to the issue, then something else is still needed, namely a criterion for objectivity. The sciences, we may admit, are paradigm instances of an objective discipline, but it is still necessary to know which of their features grant them this status. If we do not know this then we cannot tell whether the features which history admittedly lacks are just those required for objectivity.

One move which it is tempting to make in response to this request for a criterion would be to *stipulate* that the differences so far noted provide the standard for objectivity. History, then, as a subject which does not meet this standard is in a way stipulated to be subjective. But it may seem as if such a move is wholly arbitrary. Surely arguments cannot be won, or conclusions properly established, by a stipulative fiat of this kind. And it is true that if such a move is made, then the original argument is left just as it was before. For in the original argument what was at issue was a conclusion drawn from the accepted data about the differences between the disciplines. If it now appears that the conclusion says no more than the data, then it is plain that there can be no disagreement and no argument. If it is to be simply stipulated that to be objective is to have those features of natural science which history lacks, then it is plain that history is subjective. But this is not what was at issue in the original argument, and so no progress has been made in that context. The effect of such a move is rather like that of two chess players agreeing a draw, or deciding to abandon the game.

Yet the move made in stipulating a sense for 'objective' is not entirely arbitrary. For it is natural to think of the most developed sciences as not only embodying, but actually setting, certain standards of achievement. No doubt such a respectable background belief tempted Descartes to the less reputable recommendation that those standards ought to be copied in other areas of enquiry. Here there is no question of recommending any model to be copied outside the natural sciences, but only of recommending a standard with which to evaluate such other disciplines. But in that case we may deny that such a standard is one of objectivity, and say instead that it represents variously standards of exactness or precision, or generality, or predictive power, or certainty. Clearly the role of measurement in the natural sciences and their ability to express measurable relationships in the precise language of mathematics demonstrate a standard of exactness which is rarely present in history. If we choose to have one word to mark these assorted virtues, then it is perhaps tempting to use the term 'objective' for the purpose. But then the term has lost any independent sense, and functions simply as a portmanteau word for the range of qualities identified.

It is a mark of the confusion generated by the term 'objective' that in this suggested use it can have a comparative form. To say of a claim in some discipline that it is more objective than another would be to say that the former is more precise, or more general, or more powerful in prediction, or more certain. Yet it is by no means clear that in the original argument the term was being used in that way. On the contrary it may seem clear that originally there was no question of degrees of objectivity, but only of the description of particular claims as either objective or not. Such a point brings out forcibly enough the obscurity in the criteria for objectivity, and the need to provide and clarify such criteria.

Anyone who tries to think what such a criterion should be will soon discover that there are any number of distinct candidates. Perhaps to be objective a claim must command universal acceptance, or at least be accepted by most experts in the field. It is easy to see that on such a test many claims in natural science will not be objective. But the most natural candidate is that referred to in the suggestion (p. 45 fn) that one cannot be right (or wrong) about Virgil or James VI and I. For this implies that a claim is objective if and only if it is in principle able to be assessed as true or false. In this use there is no room for comparative forms of 'objective'; and although scientific claims will generally be thought of as satisfying the criterion there will be many non-scientific claims which also satisfy it. Claims such as 'Ribofilio will win the Derby' belong to no natural science but have nevertheless a decisive test for their truth or falsity. But it would make no sense on this criterion to raise the question whether such a claim was more or less objective than 'James VI and I was the son of Mary Queen of Scots'.

To be objective in this sense is not the same as being known to be true or false. If we accept the claim 'Ribofilio will win the Derby' as objective at all, then it is objective even before we know the result of the race. But we should not expect every objective claim to have so decisive and crucial a test. Any complex objective claim, whether scientific or not, may involve a number of separate considerations, some of which may be satisfied and others not in a particular case. There may be no simple observable event, like a horse race, which decides the matter one way or the other, but only a question of the balance of probability tipping one way rather than the other. The detective may mount an irrefutable case against the accused even though there is no 'direct' test of his guilt. The doctor may rightly diagnose and cure an illness even though some of the tests do not support his diagnosis. These claims satisfy the suggested criterion so long as we accept that they are in principle able to be assessed in terms of truth or falsity. If the criterion is not allowed such latitude, then certainly many scientific claims will also have to be regarded as subjective.

These points reveal a range of ambiguity even in the favoured criterion, and this should confirm a fundamental suspicion of the whole distinction between subjective and objective claims. But even if the criterion is still obscure there can be no doubt that the features so far picked out to distinguish history from science do not establish history as subjective. The explanatory gap suggested that there are no specifically historical laws, and that explanations in history borrow their principles from other disciplines or from common sense. But if one concentrates on the cases where this is true there is no reason to doubt that the borrowed principles can be assessed in terms of their truth or falsity. Indeed the point suggests at once that such assessments must be able to be made within the disciplines from which those principles are borrowed. If military strategy tells us that anyone in such a position would give the order to retreat this presumably is assessed as true rather than false within that discipline. Even common-sense principles are presumably open to assessment of some kind. No doubt it is the fate of common sense in history, as in other disciplines, to give way to a more exact or technical wisdom. But this, far from showing that such explanations are subjective, precisely demonstrates how they may be assessed as false or inadequate.

In a similar way the factual gap undoubtedly reflects something of the special character of history but does not establish it as subjective. Historians may on occasion lack crucial evidence in a way which cannot be remedied by setting up an experiment. There is, trivially, no hope at all of merely waiting for the opportunity directly to observe controversial past events. But scientists also are subject to such limitations. An experimental test which would be crucial may be technically impossible. In many areas of natural science it is not possible directly to observe the events in question. These considerations put the argument into perspective, but there is a more decisive objection to it. Even where the historical facts are not, or not yet, known the claims about them need not be subjective on the favoured criterion. To admit that a historian in a particular case may fail to find the data he directly needs is not to say that his final judgment is subjective. If he reaches a verdict at all then it must be in terms of indirect evidence which is in principle open to assessment. A historian in such a position is merely like a detective who might find his task easier if he got a confession or witnessed the crime himself, but who is still capable of identifying the murderer even without such help. Again it may be that such situations are more frequent in, or more typical of, history than natural science, but though this may be an important truth about the former it still does not establish subjectivity on the present criterion.

These lines of argument may now be seen as wrong in principle and not just wrong in detail. What would be needed on the favoured criterion to show that history is subjective are cases of general explanatory principles or particular claims which cannot be assessed in terms of truth or falsity at all. But however much the factual and explanatory gaps may show important differences between history and natural science, they do not point to cases of this kind. Of course, these moves do not exhaust the possible lines in this variation. Other criteria for objectivity might be proposed, or other differences pointed out between history and the sciences.

Nevertheless though these lines are inadequate something may be learned from them. For one thing they have made clear how necessary it is to specify as clearly as possible the criteria for objectivity which are to be applied to history. The arguments reveal how much confusion can be generated by the original contrast, and even suggest that such confusion may scarcely be worth remedying. Again, in the light of this confusion, the arguments suggest that it may be more fruitful to pursue an independent enquiry into the nature of historical study, without being driven to a conclusion about the discipline's objectivity or lack of it. In this way the analysis may be therapeutic; it may encourage us to abandon the original task in favour of that more fruitful independent enquiry.

Variation 2. Bias and prejudice

In this variation it is claimed that the historian is residually but inevitably biassed in his work, and that this is the ground for regarding history as a subjective discipline. As in the first variation we shall find that the key terms require some clarification, but the same criterion for objectivity will continue to be used. First some natural but weak arguments will be considered, in which the idea of 'bias' is used in an ordinary sense. Finally some more fruitful lines of argument will be discussed in which the same term seems to acquire a more extended use.

It is sometimes thought that historians show a bias in their choice of a topic to study, and that this introduces a subjective element into their work. But such a move is a very weak continuation. For historians, like any other investigators, inevitably choose a limited range of history to study. A historian who claimed to be studying history as a whole, and not some particular part of it, would have said something as unintelligible as a physicist who claimed to be studying physical phenomena as a whole rather than any particular aspect of such phenomena through some specific branch of physics. It is not just that such studies seem too comprehensive and unmanageable, but that they are so far incoherent. Historians inevitably select a period, or aspect of a period, in just the way in which physicists choose a topic or aspect of a topic for their research. It could not, of course, be denied that historians and physicists may make such a choice in terms of their subjective preferences or even prejudices. But this is not necessarily a complaint, and does not mean that what they then write will itself be biassed or prejudiced. A judge may have preferred to hear a case of robbery rather than one of murder, but such a preference does not mean that his conduct of the former case was biassed or prejudiced.

Nevertheless there is an improvement to be found in this line of argument. Perhaps the important point is not that the historian's initial choice may reflect his own tastes or preferences, but that his handling of the topic may be determined by his background beliefs, or principles, or values. A Soviet economic historian might produce a different account of post-war economic history from an American economic historian, even though we might insist that both are dealing with the same aspect of the same period. Differences such as these are often appealed to in advancing the view that history is ultimately subjective. Sometimes it is even suggested that similar differences may arise from the different ages in which historians live.

The historian, it may be said, subscribes inevitably to the background views of his own society and his own time, and these distort his judgment even without his being aware of it. It is easy to see how the argument might be extended from the influences of an age or a society or a class to those of individual temperament or personality. Since in the argument the historian will be unaware of these background influences, and in any case cannot overcome them, his history and that of his age and society will inevitably be coloured by such a background, just as though he viewed the selected events through tinted lenses.

It is easy to be carried away by the force of such rhetoric. Certainly such arguments do not entitle us to draw all the tempting conclusions about the uniquely subjective character of history. An eighteenth-century historian, for example, could not have written economic history in the way that a twentieth-century author may. But this does not show that the eighteenth-century writers were biassed. It may show that they did not write economic history at all, or that their efforts to do so were severely limited by ignorance of economics. It is a logical truth that a historian of one age cannot write history with resources which became available only later; but for just that reason the limitation is not peculiar to historians. Or again, in the case of a disagreement between Soviet and American economic historians the conflict appears to lie not in some elusive area of ideological values but within the discipline of economics itself. But whether that is true or not, at least the example shows that such conflicts are not unique to history but can be found in other disciplines as well. Nevertheless since this general line is so common and tempting, and since it can produce a dizzying scepticism about historical objectivity, it needs to be examined more closely as does the notion of bias itself.

There are two ways in which we may talk of bias. We may, for example, speak of a historian as biassed but we may also speak of a text as biassed. Though these uses are related they are also distinct. A historian may have a bias or prejudice in favour of some historical character, and yet be quite impartial in treating him in his text. Equally a text may be distorted even though the author himself genuinely has no prior prejudices to account for this. One relation between these two may be shown by noting that we may explain a textual bias precisely by adverting to the author's bias in the same direction. But if this is so, then it seems that bias in the personal sense cannot be a crucial item in the general argument at all. For although it is true that a historian may yield to prejudice in overlooking or disregarding evidence, or in giving a one-sided picture of some event or person, there are many other ways of producing the same sort of distortion. A man may overlook evidence not because he is prejudiced or biassed, but because he is incompetent, or blind, or careless. For this reason there is no merit in concentrating on personal bias rather than on any of the other numerous stimuli to error. What seems important in the argument is not the state of mind which may induce and account for error, so much as the kind of error in the text which might show that history is in that respect subjective.

But this admission leads to a decisive move in this variation. The criterion accepted for a claim's being subjective was that it was not able to be assessed in terms of truth or falsity. But when we speak of bias or distortion in a text we already presuppose that an error, a detectable error, has been committed. But if such errors are able to be detected, then far from establishing the subjective nature of history the argument actually demonstrates its objectivity. There would be no point or justification in speaking of error or of bias in this way unless it were possible in principle to show that a mistake had been committed. But this, far from showing an absence of standards of assessment actually presupposes just such standards.

In one way this move returns the argument from the second variation back to the first. For it reminds us that the crucial evidence for subjectivity is to be found in the text rather than in the historian's state of mind. But it also recalls a connection between the two variations in terms of the kind of claims which seem to be natural candidates for subjectivity. In the first variation it was suggested that the argument might turn on the location of explanatory principles which were incapable of being assessed as true or false. In the second it is suggested that the historian brings to his study a range of background principles, perhaps prejudices, which deserve to be called subjective. Now it might be claimed that it is in this area of background principles governing history that the discipline's subjectivity is to be located. Historians no doubt approach their chosen periods with fundamental categories and principles which may not always be clearly acknowledged or fully understood. Some of these will simply reflect the current state of theory in other disciplines, such as economics or sociology, which are relevant to the enquiry. Others may reflect a more personal or common-sense view of human life and institutions. But in all these cases it is tempting to see the historian as a prisoner of his background, inevitably succumbing to the undetected distortions of these basic principles.

It is worth making two final points here to put this thesis into perspective. First, of course, the idea of such a background and its role in ordering the historians' data remains disagreeably vague. Nevertheless it would be very surprising if the same idea did not also have application in other disciplines than history. Any natural science certainly imposes a distinctive view of its subject-matter, which could be traced back to its fundamental categories and principles. Just because they are fundamental, their assessment and their replacement cannot be as straightforward as that of less important derivative principles (see p. 40). No doubt it is this difficulty which encourages the view that such background principles are subjective. But even if that claim were accepted history would so far share its subjectivity with almost all other subjects including the natural sciences. But it would in any case be wrong simply to assume that there was no way of assessing or replacing such fundamental principles.

It may be that history has elements in its background which are unique; and that some of its explanatory principles really are subjective on the favoured criterion. But before such a claim could be accepted the idea of such a background structure, and the distinct elements which may be included in it, need more clarification. We may need at least to separate certain fundamental presuppositions, for example the logic, of the subject from its basic explanatory principles, and these in turn from any principles of value which it may contain. We should consider whether history can be treated as a unified discipline in this way like a natural science, or whether its fragmentation into different schools makes this impossible. Once again, as in the earlier variation we are left with a plea for further examination of these lines of enquiry. The original issue has no doubt the merit of unearthing them, but they have an interest quite independent of their origin.

The second point concerns the sceptical development of the argument. Those who wish to see the historian as a blind prisoner of the influences of his class, or his society, or his personality will be tempted to locate here the residual subjectivity of the discipline. If it is pointed out that such influences are open to exposure by contemporaries or successors, then the claim may be made that it is impossible to detect and eradicate all such distortions. One generation may correct the judgments of an earlier school, but it may seem inevitable that no generation could ever be wholly free from such limitations. The judgments of one man, or one class, or one time are always open to correction by another. But even the optimist who sees progress in the repudiation of earlier mistakes may reflect pessimistically that history can never be free from such error or bias. Perhaps it is here, in a kind of cosmic scepticism, that the residual subjectivity of history is located. But the claim is surely unconvincing. It relies on an idea which may be useful to historians, but which is strictly an illusion, namely that of the definitive history. Just as a scientist may dream of the definitive physics, or a completed chemistry, so historians may be inspired by the ideal of a definitive history. Like the illusions of perspective this fictitious goal may have a value, but its use in the present argument is wholly spurious. The kind of scepticism it encourages is not peculiar to history; nor is it, in the historical context, a limitation it makes sense to complain of.

Once again it is necessary to stress the incompleteness of these exploratory lines. We are in the position of the chess analyst who examines an opening variation and finds that the main lines are inadequate, but who knows that other continuations may produce improvements and that even the inadequate lines may win over the board. But the principal deficiency here is not so much in the continuation of this argument as in the independent search for answers to new questions which the enquiry has unearthed. The questions whether there are any distinctively historical explanations, what elements are contained in history's background structure, or how exactly the subject differs from the natural sciences will interest anyone who wishes to understand history better. The stock response to the original question certainly conceals these further questions and is to that extent obscurantist. But we have seen enough to recognise that it embodies also understandable motives on the part of historians. One motive for succumbing to it would be the wish to separate history from the exact sciences, to stress the creative or imaginative or humane side of historical studies. Such a motive is far from discreditable and has plainly some truth in it. But if what has been said so far is right, then it provides only a confused ground for the stock response. One may sympathise with the motive without accepting the claim in which it finds expression.

The point of this enquiry was less to give an answer to the original question than to exhibit a fragment of philosophical argument. The issue may not be entirely typical of philosophical tasks, and yet be valuable in drawing attention to some distinctive features of philosophical enquiry. Particularly, since the issue concerns another discipline as a whole, we may expect to begin to see something of a relationship between philosophy and other subjects. Further we may use the illustration to test such claims as that philosophical issues or questions are quite insulated from other subjects, that they are second-order, or linguistic in nature, and not concerned with matters of fact, or that they are therapeutic or unanswerable or nonsensical. We shall find that even in this case there often is some point in these descriptions, but that to offer them as general truths without strong qualifications can be only misleading.

It is quite clear, for example, that there is some reason to regard the original question as second-order. The question has to do with history but it is not a historical question. No doubt it is partly for this reason that historians tend to contrast it with their own enquiries and to shy away from it because it is philosophical. But it would be quite wrong to infer from this admitted truth that the philosophical issue is linguistic and not a matter of fact; and equally wrong to infer that it is quite insulated from the tasks of historians.

What gives a certain linguistic flavour to the philosophical arguments is the amount of preliminary clarification evidently needed for the original question and the key terms in it. It might be said that the original question was imperfectly understood, and could be answered only after such necessary clarification. This undoubtedly provides another ground for treating the question as philosophical. But it is hard to understand how a philosopher might think of his task as restricted to such a preliminary analysis, or of the questions uncovered by it as anything but questions of fact. Once the term 'objective' has been given a definite sense the question whether history is objective is simply a question of fact. This is even more true of some of the subsidiary questions unearthed in the analysis, such as those involving a comparison between history and the sciences. If there were a subject called 'the history of history', or 'the sociology of history', it would also be second-order in the sense so far accepted, but nobody would think of its tasks as exclusively linguistic, non-factual, or devoted only to a preliminary clarification of its questions.

It is not hard, however, to find at least two motives for holding such restrictive beliefs about the philosophical questions. First it might be said that the original philosophical question has been shown to have no clear sense, to be a non-question which cannot properly be asked at all. If this were true, then certainly there would be no further task to perform apart from the preliminary analysis which revealed such nonsense. It is easy to see how an emphasis on such a view may suggest both that philosophical questions are typically meaningless, and that philosophical tasks are purely therapeutic, designed only to reveal the question's defects so that it may no longer be asked. And it is true that the analysis even suggested at some points a range of more fruitful questions about history with which the original question might be replaced. But there was no suggestion that the original question was incapable of being answered. The analysis also made quite clear exactly what was needed to provide an answer, namely a criterion for objectivity. Even if the original question was ambiguous, still the clarification was designed as much to overcome the handicap as to underline it. The clarification in this context, as in any other, was required not in order to abandon the question but in order to provide answers to it.

Second, however, it might be said that once the questions of fact about history are made clear, then it is the business of historians to answer them. But this is no more than a half truth. Certainly there is no reason why historians should not contribute to the answers, simply because they have first-hand experience of the practice and data of history. But they are in no privileged position when it comes to a comparison between history and science, unless they happen also to have first-hand experience of the sciences as well. In classifying or analysing the structure of historical or scientific enquiry what is needed is a minimum background terminology with which to mark significant features. But such a terminology is not part of the normal vocabulary of the historian. It is difficult to resist the Cartesian view that such questions, arising between departmental disciplines, call for expertise different from that of the departmental enquiries themselves. Earlier it was suggested that these were philosophical and not historical questions. Now it might be added that they are nevertheless both philosophers' and historians' questions. The attempt to allocate such questions exclusively to one discipline or another simply breaks down.

4

FACT AND LANGUAGE

Philosophical tasks have sometimes been separated from other, especially scientific, tasks on the ground that the latter are concerned only with ground-floor facts and the former only with language. The quotation from Peters (p. 14) seemed to express such a view, in which the two kinds of enquiry are represented as excluding each other. Even by itself to distinguish a concern with facts from a concern with language seems to mark at least a difference of topic; but when this is supplemented by the belief that factual enquiries are first-order while linguistic enquiries are second-order, then these tasks may seem to be totally separated. Such a division clearly depends upon a sharp separation between facts and language which it is the aim of this chapter to consider. First I shall make a preliminary survey of the general contrast and then introduce one central philosophical way of drawing it. In the final two sections I shall consider some of the problems arising from the conflicting beliefs that facts are quite distinct from language and yet that there is some intimate connection between them.

It is important to recognise the elusiveness of both terms in the distinction between fact and language. The term 'fact', for example, is liable to figure in such different distinctions as those between fact and fiction, fact and theory, fact and value, or fact and language. The term 'language', too, needs to be treated with caution as the contrasts between language and speech, or between language competence and performance, show. These contrasts are not immediately relevant to the distinction between fact and language as it has concerned philosophers, but it is as well to bear them in mind. On the other side philosophers themselves have sometimes wished to isolate a class of 'basic' facts, from which all others could in principle be construc-

ted. The temptation then is to regard all the others as fictions or
constructs with a second-class status. But here the aim is not to
pick out any favoured, even if fundamental, set of facts, but only
to understand the general distinction between language on one side
and fact on the other.

It seems obvious that there is some contrast between the facts
in some context and the language in which we may recount those
facts. We think of the facts as quite distinct from what we say or
claim about them, even if we also hope for some correspondence
between these items. That our claims may be false, or bear no
relation to the facts, shows clearly where such a division exists. But
on the other side it is not hard to detect a puzzling intimacy between
these things. If we wish to inform someone of the facts we naturally
do so by using language. Even, it could be argued, there would be
no possibility of identifying facts without such a device as language.
This is not only because of the difficulties of presenting a situation
to someone, but also because even if we can confront someone with
the facts the procedure seems to require some linguistic discrimination in order to be effective. Confronting the housemaid with the
broken vase works only because she can attend to and understand
the relevant features of the situation (e.g. that the vase was not
broken yesterday). Such performances as 'attending to the relevant
features' or 'understanding the significance of a feature' themselves
seem to involve some grasp of a language. But even this point might
be thought to understate the dependence of fact upon language. It
may be wrong or misleading to talk of confronting a person with a
fact, as though facts were just like objects which can be moved from
one place to another. It makes sense to talk of moving a broken vase
from one room to another, but not to talk of transporting a fact
from one room to another.

In traditional philosophy this division and intimacy have sometimes been expressed in extravagant ways. An emphasis on the division has led to the belief that language has no particular importance
in the constitution of knowledge, for it merely records in more
permanent and communicable form the discrimination already
effected by the senses. An emphasis on the intimacy has led to the
belief that language somehow creates facts, or that human beings
somehow project their own ideas through language on to the world
and so fashion it in accordance with those ideas. Metaphors of this
striking kind rightly acknowledge a power and importance in
language. They may act as an initial antidote to that view of philosophers' interest in language which describes it as 'merely verbal'.

But for the rest such metaphors are obscure and need to be examined coolly if we are to understand philosophy's dominant, even exclusive, interest in language.

It might reasonably be said, for example, that if philosophers are interested in language, then they should be concerned with the history or grammar or phonology of natural languages. Certainly all these are legitimate linguistic enquiries but none of them would be accepted by philosophers as part of their interest. For one thing such areas of enquiry are already annexed by the various branches of linguistic study, but this is not the main reason for rejecting such studies as philosophical. The main reason is that these interests are as much factual as are any other enquiries into an empirical phenomenon. The occurrence and features of a natural language are as much facts as are chemical reactions or physiological functions. But if this is so, then such a concern with language cannot be philosophical for that has to be a concern with language which is not factual at all.

The point is worth emphasising both as a patent obscurity in the distinction between fact and language, and also as an indication of one important overlap between them. On one side what it shows is that we cannot think of the general distinction simply as an exclusive division between topics or areas of enquiry. To say, in answer to the question 'What are you investigating?', that you are investigating *facts* is not to pick out any specific area of enquiry at all. And to say in answer that you are investigating language would not normally be to reject an interest in facts. A philologist will normally be concerned both with language and with facts; indeed with the facts of some particular language. Even on the other side it is not hard to see that a scientist may be concerned both with the facts of his chosen enquiry and also with the language in which he expresses those facts. In some cases the overlap may be unimportant, when a scientist simply considers the style of his report on some experiment. But in other cases where he may have to choose between the languages involved in different branches of mathematics, or where he is called upon to revise the criteria for the application of a term, the interaction of fact and language may be highly important.

An interest in, or concern with, facts does not therefore normally exclude a concern with language. On the contrary in the cases cited the two kinds of interest naturally go hand in hand. More generally these cases indicate a large range of activities, coming under the general heading of enquiry, which will certainly involve both fact and language in some way or other. Only at the extremes, perhaps in the barest observation of a particular occurrence, in the most abstract of mathematics or logic, or in the wildest of poetic fancies, may we approach cases where either language or fact seems scarcely involved at all. Yet philosophers are supposed to be concerned with language in a way which excludes facts altogether. Nothing has so far been said to show that such a concern is impossible, but its indication of models for philosophy as diverse as mathematics and poetry shows that it is radically unclear. Evidently what is needed is an account of the ways in which philosophers represent their interests as linguistic but not factual.

1. *Factual and linguistic claims*

There are two related ways in which such a philosophical interest may be introduced. In the first of these it is shown that claims may have both factual and linguistic features; and in the second it is shown that we can distinguish certain claims in a language as factual from certain others which are linguistic. The first of these procedures relates the terms 'factual' and 'linguistic' to features of one and the same expression; the second relates these terms to different expressions in a language.

Such a claim as 'That tree is deciduous', uttered by some person on some occasion in those words, may be said to have both factual and linguistic features. The claim, we may say, expresses a fact, or at least does so when what it asserts is simply true. But even if the claim turns out to be false of the particular object referred to, this also involves a factual feature of the claim. But the claim has also many linguistic features concerning, for example, the form of words in which it is expressed, the conventions it relies on to establish reference to a particular object, or to establish the sense of the predicate ascribed to that object.

These features point to different kinds of disagreement which might arise over such a claim. If the claim is entirely unambiguous there may still be disagreements about its truth or falsity, which an expert might be allowed to settle. But it may be that the claim's truth or falsity is itself unclear either because the claim is ambiguous or because there is disagreement about its linguistic features. Two people may dispute about such a claim because one assumes that 'deciduous' means 'not coniferous' and the other assumes that the word means 'shedding leaves in the autumn'. In such a case for the disputants there can be no question of directly deciding the claim's truth or falsity, since there is no agreement about what the claim actually asserts. Disputes generally may involve both factual and linguistic considerations, as the earlier argument about history showed (Chapter 3). Even though both kinds of consideration may be distinguished it is often unclear which is mainly at issue.

The second way of introducing the terms 'factual' and 'linguistic' would be to consider not distinct features of the same claim but different kinds of claim. The claim (1) 'That tree is deciduous' may be described as factual, since its truth or falsity is determined by reference to facts. But there are other kinds of claim whose truth or falsity may be determined not by facts but rather by the linguistic conventions which govern the sense of its constituent terms. If, for example, we formulate these conventions in the case of (1), then we obtain something like a definition to the effect that 'deciduous' means 'shedding leaves in the autumn'. But in that case the claim (2) 'Deciduous trees shed their leaves in the autumn' will have its truth determined by the meanings of its constituents, and by the conventions which establish those meanings. The conventions which played only a part in helping to establish the truth or falsity of (1) here fully determine the truth or falsity of (2). It is convenient to use the notions of necessary and contingent truth (or falsity) to mark this distinction between type (2) claims whose truth or falsity is fully determined by a linguistic convention and type (1) claims whose truth or falsity is not so determined. We may then say that the claim 'That tree is deciduous' is a contingent (factual) truth; and that the claim 'Deciduous trees shed their leaves in the autumn' is a necessary (linguistic) truth.

This kind of distinction has come under heavy philosophical fire.[1] It has been argued, for example, that no adequate general account of linguistic conventions has yet been given, which would enable us to draw the distinction with confidence in all cases. It has been argued that it would be unjustified to extend this account of necessary truth to cover other cases such as the propositions of mathematics. And it has been argued that we may come to accept a necessary truth by appealing to empirical evidence.

These criticisms, however, are not directed at the account so far given, but rather at certain extensions of the account which are not here being advanced. The account so far given is not committed, for example, to the view that every claim can be demonstrably fitted into one or other of these categories; nor is it committed to the view that

---

[1] See W. V. O. Quine, 'Two Dogmas of Empiricism', reprinted in the author's *From a Logical Point of View* (2nd ed., Harvard, 1964); R. M. Chisholm, *Theory of Knowledge* (New Jersey, 1966), p. 83; and J. A. Bernadete, 'Sense-perception and the *A Priori*', *Mind*, April 1969.

C

our understanding and identification of linguistic conventions cannot be improved. Equally, nothing has been said to deny that we might accept a necessary truth on the basis of empirical evidence. For it is not claimed that the only way of coming to hold such claims is by appealing to a prior linguistic convention. All that is claimed is that if such a convention is established, then a corresponding necessary truth will also be established. Nothing, too, has been said to deny that there may be other necessary truths, for example in mathematics, which are not exactly of this simple kind. Such points as these are not so much criticisms of the account as helpful aids to understanding it; they do not constitute objections to the account so much as reminders of its possible limitations.

To evade such difficulties is, however, not much of a recommendation, and it may be useful therefore to stress a more positive merit in the account. It offers in place of a substantival contrast between fact and language an adjectival distinction between various items of a factual or a linguistic kind. At least such a grammatical shift may prevent us from hypostatising the terms in the original distinction. More importantly the new formulation may remind us of the variety of items to which the adjectives may be applied. We may speak, for example, of factual or linguistic enquiries, of factual or linguistic claims, of factual or linguistic disputes, or principles or changes. There is no reason to think that the adjectives function in exactly the same way in these different contexts.

It might be thought, for example, that a distinction between factual and linguistic enquiry can be explained in terms of the contrast between factual and linguistic claims. For it might seem obvious that factual enquiries result in factual claims, and that linguistic enquiries produce linguistic claims. Yet to say this is to run a risk of serious confusion. It has been pointed out already that it is possible for factual and linguistic considerations to overlap in an enquiry. Descartes' distinction between perfectly and imperfectly understood questions (Chapter 2) pointed to the possibility of prior clarification in an enquiry whether or not it is ultimately directed to matters of fact. And the enquiry into history (Chapter 3) clearly involved both questions of meaning and questions of fact. No doubt it is a matter of fact that a particular vehicle has a certain momentum. But in the eighteenth century when it was unclear how momentum should be measured, such an issue involved not only facts but also the conventions governing the term 'momentum'. On the other side, too, it has been pointed out that many enquiries rightly called linguistic are also indisputably factual. An enquiry into the history or phonology of a natural language may correctly be described both as linguistic and as factual.

In relation to enquiries, it seems, the two adjectives 'factual' and 'linguistic' do not exclude each other. Yet in the context of claims, where we distinguish contingent (factual) from necessary (linguistic) truth, the terms are exclusive. Hence it would be a confusion to infer directly from the belief that philosophers are concerned with linguistic claims that their enquiries are linguistic and not factual, or vice versa. Not only do the terms function differently with respect to exclusiveness, but they also have different senses in the two contexts. In the sense in which the terms apply to claims they could not be applied to enquiries at all. For it makes no sense to speak of enquiries as true or false, still less as contingently or necessarily true or false.

It is tempting to suggest that such a confusion may have led some philosophers to hold that factual considerations are irrelevant to philosophy; or to distinguish science as a factual enquiry from philosophy as linguistic; or to claim that questions of meaning are precisely opposed to, or separated from, questions of fact. It would be right to hesitate more before offering such a diagnosis if there were not in the philosophical revolution a long history of belief in a non-factual semantics to which philosophers contribute. Perhaps it was some such background which led Schlick to say 'There can be no science of meaning, because there cannot be any set of true propositions about meaning'; or which led Moore to distinguish his own enquiries into meaning from those of lexicographers.[1] The idea that semantic features alone among aspects of language may or must be treated non-factually is an inevitable temptation for anyone who holds that philosophers are concerned with meaning and not with fact. Of course it may still be possible to attach another sense to the phrase 'linguistic enquiry' in which it is quite separated from questions of fact. It may be urged, for example, that mathematical enquiry is of this kind. In the next section more will be said of the attempt to separate fact and language in this way.

2. *Three kinds of language*

There are at least three different ways in which we may think of languages. On one side the natural languages, English or French, provide paradigm examples of language, in which a reference to the words or expressions of the language is essential. Languages which

---

[1] M. Schlick, 'The Future of Philosophy'; G. E. Moore, *Principia Ethica* (Cambridge, 1903), ch. 1.

have this feature may be called 'notation-bound'. But there are also other ways in which we may talk of the languages of mathematics or chess or love. Sometimes such a usage may reflect only a difference between syntax and vocabulary within a natural language. Thus 'the language of chess' may mean no more than 'the vocabulary of chess in English', and so refer only to a part of a natural language. But we may also, in speaking of the language of mathematics or of chess intend rather to identify the claims made in these contexts, irrespective of any natural language or notation. A Russian who knows no German may nevertheless understand the language of mathematics just as well as a German who knows no Russian. Here to know the language is to understand certain ideas or concepts, however they may be expressed; it approximates to being a competent practitioner of the relevant discipline.

It may be thought that we speak in this way of the language of mathematics only because there is a notation for the subject quite independent of natural languages. But that this is not the crucial feature of the case can be seen in the other example of a chess language. For there is no extensive symbolism for talking about games of chess independently of natural languages. Even the algebraic notation for recording games, which contains only a small part of what should be included in the chess language, often employs natural language symbols for the pieces. If in this case we say of two people who understand only their own distinct natural languages that they nevertheless both understand the language of chess, then such a language cannot be identified with any natural language and must be notation-free. It is a somewhat curious consequence of this usage that two such people may be unable to communicate with each other, even about chess, just because they do not share a common notation with which to express their views, even though they speak the same language.

A language in this second sense is parasitic upon other ways of identifying languages. We may speak of a notation-free language only on the basis of some notation which is already available to us. We can transcend notation in this way only by availing ourselves of it. We might, for example, speak of a class of notation-free claims based on those expressible in some natural language such as English. The language that we then identify is based upon a notation-bound natural language, but covers also any claims expressed in other natural languages which may be translated into English. Or, alternatively, we may think of a language in the second sense as covering claims made about a particular topic, area of enquiry, or practice.

It is for this reason that we naturally think of technical systems such as those of mathematics, physics, chess, or law as involving languages in this second sense.

It is, consequently, easy to slip from this second sense of 'language' to a third in which the term stands rather for a theory, or discipline, or practice. If we think of technical systems such as mathematics or physics or law as involving languages in the notation-free sense, then we may also come to think of those languages as identical with such systems. We may come to think of the language of physics, for example, as containing only those claims, however expressed, which are currently accepted within the discipline. Earlier it was suggested that understanding a language in the second sense might approximate to being a competent practitioner of the relevant discipline. A man who could merely construct sentences about number or about chess but who was quite unable to do mathematics or play chess might not be allowed to know the languages of mathematics or chess. But it is easy to see in some cases that a language in the second sense includes much more than the claims currently accepted within an area of enquiry. Such a language based on English, for example, will include all the claims expressible in the natural language including many pairs of incompatible claims. Analogously the language of physics or chess might be taken to include all the claims in that context expressed by sentences which are grammatically and semantically well formed, even though many of these are known to be false. But a mathematical system, physical theory, or code of law could not properly contain incompatible elements, or large numbers of claims known to be false.

There are also other overlaps between languages in these different senses. A linguist who formulates rules to generate all and only well-formed, acceptable, expressions in English may be said to have constructed a theory. For his account of the structure of the natural language may be tested by its adequacy in generating such expressions in English. But if the theory were acceptable, then we might also say that his rules constitute or identify the language itself. Such an overlap occurs because in this case the acceptability of a theory is tied to linguistic acceptability. The theory is a theory about what is required to generate linguistically acceptable expressions in English. In a similar way it may be claimed that mathematical systems are themselves languages, since the acceptability of expressions within the system is wholly determined by its stipulated conventions. The generation of truths in such systems appears analogous to the generation of linguistically acceptable expressions in a natural language. We may further be disinclined to speak of mathematical systems as theories, if we reserve the term 'theory' for empirically testable systems. Yet it is plain that the analogy with the generation of expressions in a natural language is not exact. For in mathematics what are generated are only expressions which are necessarily true, and not all well-formed expressions.

It is the second, parasitic, sense of 'language' as notation-free which has mainly interested philosophers. In this account one and the same language may be expressed in innumerably different words or expressions. Philosophers, with an interest in the meanings of expressions rather than in the expressions which convey that meaning, have made the same distinction at a lower level between sentences and propositions. Sentences belong properly to notation-bound languages, but the propositions expressed by them are common to any languages which can translate those sentences. Some philosophers, notably Quine,[1] have wanted to eliminate any reference to propositions, but it is easy to see one motive behind their introduction. It often is useful to talk of the meaning of expressions independently of the particular language or notation in which the meaning happens to be expressed. If there are problems at all expressed in the questions, 'Is history objective?', or 'Can there be a non-factual semantics?' then they arise just as much whether they are formulated in English, French, or any other language.

Nevertheless there is no doubt that the terminology may be misleading. In particular, it is tempting to think that such a device lifts the philosophical interest in meaning above the realm of natural or notation-bound language. And it is, as a consequence, tempting to think of a domain of concepts and propositions, separated from mere words and sentences, which is available for philosophical inspection without empirical enquiry. Perhaps few philosophers in the revolution explicitly followed such a Platonic line of thought, and yet this is one possible way in which a philosophical interest in language may come to be distinguished, even insulated, from the empirical enquiries of linguists and lexicographers. The quotations from Schlick, Moore and Peters indicate how tempting and pervasive has been the philosophical separation of language from fact.

In the work of two philosophers in the revolution, Moore and Wisdom, this issue formed a central theme. Moore wished explicitly to distinguish his semantic enquiries from those of lexicographers, and spoke of his analysis of propositions as independent of natural

[1] e.g. W. V. O. Quine, *The Philosophy of Logic* (New Jersey, 1969), contains a typical and sustained attack upon the terminology of propositions.

language.[1] Moore's positive views about the nature of his philosophical analysis are complex, but there can be no doubt that he sometimes thought of analysis as directed to a domain of concepts or propositions quite insulated from any features of a natural language. Wisdom, by contrast, found it impossible to make such a strong separation between philosophy and lexicography. He was prepared to concede that philosophers' claims about language could be shown to be false by appealing to linguistic usage. Nevertheless he held that philosophers and linguists approached their common ground from quite different directions. Linguists were merely concerned with the accuracy of their claims about usage, but philosophers were concerned not with accuracy so much as insight or linguistic penetration. In order to produce such insight philosophers may recommend, or indulge in, usages which violate existing linguistic conventions. When a philosopher takes the sceptical view that we never *know* truths about material objects, though we may know truths of mathematics, he undoubtedly violates the ordinary use of the word 'know'. But the point of such a violation is to draw our attention to differences between the truths of mathematics and those about material objects.[2]

The strong separation of fact from language is open to decisive objections. Though it is natural for philosophers to think of notation as relatively unimportant beside the meanings expressed in it, this by no means establishes that enquiry into meaning can be wholly independent of notation. It is true that to speak of propositions, or of language in the notation-free sense, is to avoid any particular notation, but such a device cannot free us from every notation. To say that no particular natural language is involved in some analysis, is not to say that every natural language can be dispensed with. On the contrary, some notation or natural language is necessary in order to identify the propositions to be analysed. Moore's perfectly correct premiss that his problems could be expressed indifferently in any number of natural languages did not entitle him to conclude that he had no concern with natural language at all. It may be true,

[1] See, for example, Moore, op. cit., p. 6: 'If I wanted that (lexicographical) kind of definition I should have to consider in the first place how people generally used the word "good"; but my business is not with its proper usage as established by custom.' See also A. White, *G. E. Moore* (Oxford, 1958), chs. IV, V, and VI.
[2] See, for example, J. Wisdom, 'Philosophical Perplexity', reprinted in *Philosophy and Psycho-Analysis* (Oxford, 1953), p. 41: 'Philosophical theories are illuminating . . . when they suggest, or draw attention to, a terminology which reveals likenesses and differences concealed by ordinary language.' See also 'Ostentation', op. cit., pp. 6–7; and 'Is Analysis a Useful Method in Philosophy?', op. cit., p. 16.

on a cross-channel boat, that goods may be bought indifferently with English, or Belgian, or French currency, but it cannot be inferred from this that goods may be bought without any currency at all.

Hence, as Wisdom acknowledged, there must be some overlap between philosophers' and linguists' claims about meaning. A non-factual semantics in the strong sense is quite incoherent. Yet Wisdom's attempt to separate the intentions or insights of philosophers and linguists is not itself satisfactory. For one thing it implies that all philosophical issues are linguistic or sceptical in nature, though such views are quite unplausible. But even for the area of philosophy they identify Wisdom's account fails to distinguish the status of necessary truths from that of the conventions which establish them. When he raised the question 'Does (1) "A monarchy is a set of people under a king" mean the same as (2) " 'Monarchy' means the same as 'Set of people under a king' "?' his answer was that either view could be taken, so long as one was careful.[1] Yet, as we have seen, there are good reasons for distinguishing type (1) necessary truths from type (2) conventions. Type (2) claims form the basis for the special status of type (1) claims. The former provide just that necessary reference to a notation-bound language which type (1) claims do not explicitly make. It is for just these reasons that type (2) claims cannot themselves be regarded as necessary truths, since their truth is not determined by any prior semantic conventions. To overlook these differences is inevitably to encourage a belief in a non-factual semantics. For if type (2) claims were themselves necessary truths, then it may indeed look as though claims about the meanings of words had no need of empirical enquiry, and were not vulnerable to any factual tests.

So far the attempt to separate language and fact in philosophy, in order to justify a non-factual interest in language, seems unsuccessful. But there are two further moves that might still be made to support the attempt. In the first of these it might be said that philosophical claims are essentially of type (1), that is, are necessary truths. Such claims would be non-factual in that their truth or falsity may be determined by reference to linguistic conventions. The assertion of such claims still has a remote connection with facts, for in the natural language model it is by reference to facts that the linguistic conventions are themselves established. But if there were an enquiry which consisted in the generation of necessary truths without reference to prior facts of usage, then it could be regarded as linguistic and non-factual. It has, indeed, already been suggested that such enquiries are associated with disciplines like mathematics. And it was pointed out earlier (p. 33) that such a view of philosophy offered one way of rehabilitating the subject in the revolution. So, it might be said, just as mathematics contains necessary truths about number, generated from a set of conventions, so philosophy may contain necessary truths about meaning. If the analogy were right, then there would be some room for a non-factual semantics.

The second, related, way of supporting the attempt was already present in Wisdom's account. For there it was acknowledged that philosophers may wish not merely to record current usage, as lexicographers do, but to recommend or stipulate changes in it. Clearly a conscious recommendation to alter the meaning of some expression, formulated in a type (2) convention, cannot be vulnerable to facts of existing usage. If it were, then every linguistic innovation would be condemned from the start. In a somewhat similar way it may be claimed that the background conventions of the sciences, or mathematics, or any technical field, are not vulnerable to facts of ordinary usage. Such conventions may embody deliberate deviations from current technical or non-technical usage. So philosophers also may escape from those facts of usage so long as they offer their type (2) claims not as records of current speech but as recommending or stipulating alternatives to it. These views will be considered at the end of the next section after a discussion of an alleged intimacy between fact and language.

3. *Language and the creation of fact*
At the end of A. J. Ayer's 1960 inaugural lecture he wrote,

Finally whatever view one may take of the more specialised interests of linguistic philosophy, there still remains the problem of elucidating the concept of language itself. One of the debts we owe to Wittgenstein, and before him to the Pragmatists, is a realisation of the active part that language plays in the constitution of facts. If 'the world is everything that is the case', then what can be the case depends upon our conceptual system.

Such claims acknowledge both an unclarity in the notion of a language, and also an intimacy between language and fact, which might extravagantly be put by speaking of a language as in some way creating or constituting facts. So far what has been emphasised in resisting the sharp philosophical separation of fact from language is the way in which facts have a bearing on claims about meaning in a natural language. But the relationship to which Ayer refers is plainly of a quite new kind. For it suggests that linguistic conventions may sometimes look not only backwards to facts for their support, but also forwards to the very constitution of the facts themselves.

The most obvious examples of such an intimacy come from the area of prescriptive or practical discourse. It is primarily in these areas that philosophers have distinguished between summary and constitutive rules, and between brute and institutional facts.[1] Constitutive rules actually bring a general practice into being, or institute it, and do not merely summarise an existing activity. Institutional facts may be said to put a particular interpretation on certain brute facts in classifying them by reference to the background rules and conventions of some institution. If I invent the game of chess and promulgate rules to govern it, then I actually institute a general practice rather than merely summarise or formalise some existing activity. By contrast if after watching other people play chess I try to formulate the rules which govern their play I would be merely summarising an already existing activity. Clearly many cases will not fit simply into either classification. If after playing chess in a haphazard way I formulate the strategic principle that White's strongest opening move is P–K4 I may in some respects be reflecting and summarising the results of previous play, but I may actually be instituting a strategic theory of the game. The activity of chess playing, and innumerable descriptions of detailed acts within that framework, are made possible by the constitutive rules of the system. The brute facts relative to the institution of chess would involve a neutral vocabulary such as that of geographical movement of lumps of wood over a squared surface.

It is not hard to find other examples of such institutional conventions. One way of looking at violations of the law would be to treat them as offences to be punished. But we could choose instead to regard them as symptoms of an illness to be cured or prevented rather than punished. Just as constitutive rules may initiate a practice, so it is open to us also to amend those rules and change the practice. A particular law may be changed so that what was earlier regarded as a sufficient ground for divorce is now replaced by a quite different ground. We may cease to admit the official legal existence of matrimonial offences and choose instead to speak of the irretrievable breakdown of a marriage. In such cases it seems natural

[1] See John Rawls, 'Two Concepts of Rules', *Philosophical Review*, 1955; G. E. M. Anscombe, 'On Brute Facts', *Analysis*, 1958; J. Searle,' How to Derive "Ought" from "Is"', *Philosophical Review*, 1964.

to speak of a language in some way determining what the facts are, or of a change in the language in some way bringing about a change in the facts. Before there are chess rules we cannot perform actions describable in terms of chess playing. After the rules institute the practice it is possible for us to describe actions in this way and so to perform them. If we accept a traditional view of violations of the law we accept the concepts and apparatus of punishment and penal institutions. If we abandon such a view, and choose instead to talk in terms of sickness or deviance, then we may also have abandoned such a framework of punishment. It may not always be entirely clear what are the consequences of such changes, but it can scarcely be doubted that it is open to us to make them.

But although the phenomenon exists it is still unclear that we should describe it in terms of a language actually creating or constituting facts. For one thing, although such operations may make possible certain ranges or kinds of facts, they do not in any way determine particular facts within that range. The rules of chess enable us to describe Fischer's fourth move in his sixth match game with Petrosian in 1971, but they cannot tell us what that move was. We may think of a language as embodying a set of discriminations which divide reality up into recognisable parts. There is perhaps some general presumption in formulating a new language that its basic terms have an application. But the institution of a language by itself cannot determine whether it has application, and even if it has the language itself cannot determine any particular facts within its general range. To suppose that it could would be to obliterate any distinction between the facts and the language we use to record them. It would be to suggest that the mere invention of a language is enough to guarantee the truth of its claims. Certainly language can be said in some way to identify facts, but not in a way that is incompatible with their identification independently by observation or experiment.

It is also unclear what in this case is to count as a language. Perhaps it is possible to understand the term so that it always is due to language that such institutions are created. But without such a re-definition we could not generally infer that such institutions, though recorded in language, were also due to it. It would be quite possible to admit that a language enables us to express a range of discriminations and still claim that the language was not responsible for them. There are important differences here between the different senses of language. A language in the second sense for example could not be said to enable us to express certain discriminations, since at the level of concepts this kind of language just is nothing but a set of discriminations. But apart from that difficulty it would still be odd to ascribe responsibility for some alleviation of a harsh penal system to our language rather than to our humanitarian instincts, or some other aspects of our moral or intellectual make-up. It is natural, for these reasons, that the idea of a language may be extended to cover such general capacities, as in Chomsky's idea of a language faculty. Ayer's switch from the term 'language' to 'conceptual system' in the quotation is another example of the same tendency.

These provisos put the original claim into perspective. We may usefully admit that the formulation of conventions or principles in some area may grant official recognition to some phenomenon without claiming that the language has primary responsibility for the existence or even recognition of the phenomenon. The language may mark the official recognition, but only the independent facts determine whether there is anything to recognise. We may alter our official grounds for divorce from matrimonial offence to irretrievable breakdown of the marriage, but this still leaves it undetermined whether there really are any cases of irretrievable breakdown in existing marriages. And even if such cases exist the responsibility for their recognition in the law may not be due simply to the change of language. It is a joke, and not a very good one, to complain that it is legislators who create crimes, or the doctors' more sophisticated diagnoses which are responsible for the spread of disease.

It may be argued that these examples of practical rules cannot be matched in theoretical contexts. It is open to us to determine what counts as a crime, or whether we recognise the classification of acts as crimes at all, but, it may be said, it is not open to us to determine what counts as a metal or an elementary physical particle, or whether we recognise a classification of matter into metals or elementary particles. Yet the examples are unconvincing, and the supposed contrast between practice and theory has in any case already been undermined. We may institute not only the rules of chess but also the principles of a theory of chess. We may wish to speak of deviance rather than crime not for the practical purpose of law reform, but to institute a theory of social behaviour. No doubt doctors should not legislate arbitrarily about diseases, but it is still up to them to provide a classification for conditions which will grant or withhold official recognition to them as diseases. The official recognition which doctors and scientists grant in their theories is certainly subject to any number of constraints, but so is the official recognition that may be accorded in law to certain acts as crimes. Once it is admitted that in neither context can official recognition guarantee its own success, then the differences between the two kinds of case seem minimal. No doubt the criteria of success or failure will be different in the distinct contexts, but it would be remarkable if no such criteria existed in either area. It is not a mere accident that philosophers like Ayer and Körner should use the term 'constitutive principle' in theoretical contexts, just as Rawls did in connection with practices.[1] In the sense in which it has been so far allowed that language may constitute facts in practice, it may also do it in theory as well. But it should be remembered that the parallel is achieved only by restricting the force of such a claim in both contexts. In both kinds of case a language may embody an inventiveness in, or mark a contribution to, the recognition of facts. In neither case could it be said genuinely to create them.

But even if such a view about language can be extended in a purified form from practical to theoretical contexts there is one important respect in which it remains unclear. Although we have some idea of what constitutive principles may do, the notion of a language in which they may occur is still ambiguous. In particular, it may be said that the status of such principles will vary according to the kind of language they occur in. In the natural language model such principles may be thought of as purely semantic, but in the model in which language is seen as a kind of theory it may be assumed that at least some constitutive principles must be of a factual kind. We may assume that within the general notions of a language or of a constitutive principle a clear and exclusive division can be drawn between those principles which are strictly linguistic and those which are factual.

For the present, however, it is not possible to offer any such clear simple division. Indeed the argument so far suggests that even to expect such a sharp distinction is to expect too much. The semantic conventions of a natural language are themselves vulnerable to facts of usage. The constitutive principles of a theory may include proposals about the criteria for the application of its key terms and so contain a reference both to language and to fact. Moreover philosophers such as Quine and Pap have argued plausibly that there is no clear or exclusive distinction to be drawn within a theory between its factual and its linguistic principles.[2] In particular it has

[1] See S. Körner, *Categorial Frameworks* (Oxford, 1970).
[2] W. V. O. Quine, 'Two Dogmas of Empiricism'; A. Pap, *The A Priori in Physical Theory* (New York, 1946).

been argued that such a distinction cannot be drawn in terms of a principle's revisability in the face of recalcitrant experience. It may be thought that only factual principles would be revisable in this way, but it has been shown that such difficulties can be accommodated by altering principles that seemed not to be factual at all. To attempt to distinguish in this way between factual and linguistic principles is to fail to do justice to the complexity of theoretical systems.

We are left, then, with the idea of a background of constitutive principles governing some area of enquiry or practice. Philosophers who have wished to point to the existence of such principles even in empirical theories have sometimes called them 'conceptual' or '*a priori*' to mark their special status. But such labels, like the ambiguous alternative 'linguistic', stand rather as signposts to the task of elucidating their nature than as monuments to its successful completion. All that can be said for the present is that any area of enquiry, or theory, or practice will have such background principles. To be clear and explicit about them, to understand their function and status, are tasks that involve both the practitioners of the discipline and philosophers as well. It was, for example, such a task that began to emerge dimly from the unclarities surrounding the question about history's objectivity. They are tasks that occur in the very centre of the area in which philosophy and other disciplines overlap.

In the light of this account it should be easier to deal with the suggestions made in the previous section about philosophy's linguistic but non-factual tasks. The second suggestion was that philosophers may retain a linguistic interest and escape from facts of usage so long as they do not merely record or reflect usage but recommend changes in it. But such recommendations cannot be made quite idly, in the manner of Humpty Dumpty. If they are to have any force or value they must confer some benefit, or at least should be proposed with the aim of securing some advantage. But whatever the advantage may be, and however poorly articulated or developed such a proposal may be, it will for this reason have the status of a constitutive principle. In making such proposals philosophers will be engaging in a linguistic activity, but not in one that can be totally insulated from facts. If such a proposal is not idle or empty, then it must function at least as a proposed way of interpreting facts. If Quine is right it will, like all governing principles of a theory, be vulnerable to revision in the light of recalcitrant facts.

But it may be supposed that philosophers could avoid even this reference to fact so long as they adopted the first suggestion. There it was proposed that philosophers might confine their activities to generating necessary truths relating to meaning, in the way that mathematics generates necessary truths relating to number. But such a suggestion is simply confused. There is no reason why philosophers should not construct systems of necessary truth, as in logic and mathematics. Equally there is no reason why they should not be concerned to understand, and develop a theoretical account of, meaning. What is difficult is to see how these requirements are to be jointly satisfied in an enterprise that is linguistic but not factual. For natural language meaning is an empirical phenomenon, like other features of a natural language. It is true that the phenomenon is not a simple observable feature of human behaviour, and consequently that in order to understand it we need to construct a theory with its own constitutive principles. But such a theory, even if it is modelled on or contains elements from a logical system, is still empirical with a necessary reference at some point to the data of linguistic usage.

On the other hand, however, we may think of a linguistic enquiry not in relation simply to natural languages, but in relation to the background principles of any theory or practice. It has indeed been argued that such a task is important and typically philosophical, but it may have nothing to do with natural language meaning. Nor is it, or the principles involved in it, necessarily insulated from facts. What causes the difficulty here is the noted ambiguity arising from the term 'linguistic'. On one side it indicates a specific topic for investigation, namely natural language and especially the feature of meaning in it. But on the other side it indicates instead a functional element in a theory relating to any topic whatever. An enquiry relating to a theory of natural language meaning will be linguistic in both of these ways. Perhaps it was because of this ambiguity that philosophers have held that they should be exclusively concerned with meaning, and that their enquiries could be insulated from facts.

LANGUAGE AND PERCEPTION

Problems about perception have long exercised philosophers. They offer for that reason alone a good example of the change in approach which distinguishes traditional from revolutionary philosophy. More specifically one traditional argument in this context, the argument from illusion, was explicitly reformulated by a revolutionary philosopher in a linguistic way. In Ayer's *The Foundations of Empirical Knowledge* (London, 1940) it was argued that in this case traditional philosophers had mistaken what was a linguistic dispute for one of fact. Ayer's argument, apart from its own intrinsic interest, was also a landmark in the migration to the view that philosophical problems are essentially linguistic. For these reasons it deserves close attention. The main outlines of the argument from illusion can be simply drawn, but its ramifications are complex. The aim here is only to examine the grounds in favour of a linguistic reinterpretation of the argument, rather than to consider all its aspects.

Philosophers have traditionally asked about the relation between perception and knowledge. Some, like Locke, have suggested that all knowledge must in some way derive from sense perception. Others, like Descartes, have thought of the contribution of sense perception as either secondary or non-existent. Perhaps the two most powerful considerations in favour of the latter view lie first in the existence of knowledge, for example in mathematics, which seems to be independent of the senses, and second in the existence of perceptual illusions. The first indicates that sense perception is not necessary for knowledge, and the second that sense perception is very far from sufficient for it. Everybody recognises that their senses may deceive them, or that things do not always appear to the senses as they really are. What has distinguished philosophers from ordinary men in this context is not the degree of conviction with which they have held such views so much as the conclusions that have been drawn from them. It has, for example, sometimes been thought that because of the existence of illusions the whole of our perception is fundamentally unreliable. Descartes' metaphor of the basket containing some rotten apples, in which it is suggested that even some faulty perceptions may infect the rest, is a picturesque expression of one such inference. But our interest is in another, less dramatic but far more tempting, conclusion.

If it is the case that our senses may mislead us about the external objects we normally claim to perceive, it may seem as though those external objects cannot be directly or immediately perceived. If I see two railway lines which appear to meet in the distance, when I know that they are in fact parallel, then it may seem plausible to claim that I did not directly see the railway lines at all but something else. For what I saw evidently had a certain property of convergence which the actual railway lines do not possess. What could be more natural, then, than to suggest that in perception what we are directly aware of is an image, idea, or representation of an external object from which the existence and features of that object are inferred? Apart from the naturalness of such a locution it seems also to confer distinct benefits. For it apparently begins to explain how it is that illusions arise at all. They arise on this view because we do not perceive external objects directly, but only infer them from some intermediary representation. Because there is a convenient gap between what we directly perceive and the external objects them-selves, and because intermediaries are notoriously distorting agents, there is just that room for error which we regrettably find in the phenomenon of illusion. Hence it may seem better, more sophisti-cated and accurate, to say, what we do not ordinarily believe, that we perceive *directly* things which represent or misrepresent external objects themselves. Such directly accessible things have been variously called 'ideas', 'sensations', 'representations', or 'sense-data'.

Ayer's view is that this traditional argument is radically mis-conceived. For what it puts forward as a matter of fact is, properly understood, only a matter of language. In order to make this view clear Ayer reformulates the argument in a more precise way. The argument begins from the premiss that we sometimes have per-ceptual illusions. In these cases, it may be further asumed, we do not directly perceive an external object.[1] Now it would evidently

---

[1] This further assumption could itself be questioned, as Austin questioned it in his *Sense and Sensibilia* (Oxford, 1962), pp. 14 ff.

be a gross fallacy to infer from these premises that we *never* directly perceive external objects, even when our perception is not illusory but veridical. Additional premises are therefore needed to secure this conclusion, and Ayer notes three such premises, either of which might produce the desired result. Here only one of these three candidates will be considered, namely that formulated as

If veridical and delusive perceptions were perceptions of objects of different types, they would always be qualitatively distinguishable.

Earlier Ayer had elaborated the same principle by saying

But, it is argued, if, when our perceptions are delusive we were always perceiving something of a different kind from what we perceived when they were veridical, we should expect our experience to be qualitatively different in the two cases. We should expect to be able to tell, from the intrinsic character of the perception, whether it was a perception of a sense-datum or of a material thing.[1]

This additional premiss is not easy to understand at once, but its central function is clear. It is designed to provide a conclusive ground for likening the two cases of veridical and delusive perception. If the two cases can be shown to be similar in a relevant respect then what has been admitted in the delusive case, that in it we do not directly perceive an external object, will be true of the veridical case. Such a move would then dispose once and for all of the objection that the argument works only for delusive and not for veridical perception. In more detail the premiss attempts to assimilate the two cases by claiming that if they were not relevantly alike, then we would expect to be able to tell merely from the way things appear to us whether we were perceiving veridically or delusively. Since it is assumed that we cannot always tell merely from the way things appear whether our perception is veridical or not, it is concluded that the two cases are indeed similar in the relevant respect. But that means that in neither case do we directly perceive external objects.

Plainly even this amount of clarification is insufficient, and this is confirmed by Ayer's own attitude to the additional premiss. For, although he is critical of the traditional argument, he does not wish to reject it altogether. In particular, his criticisms are directed at the traditional belief that the premisses and conclusion of the argument are all simply matters of fact. In Ayer's view at least some of these are not matters of fact at all, but matters of language. Consequently the fault of traditional philosophers was rather to have misunder-

[1] *The Foundations of Empirical Knowledge* (London, 1940), p. 12 and p. 6.

stood the nature of the argument than to have constructed a fallacious inference. Ayer himself was prepared to accept the additional premiss and the conclusion, so long as they are rightly construed as 'rules of language'. He provides two central arguments to support this view, and it is these arguments which now need to be examined.

1. The first argument for a linguistic reinterpretation

Ayer's first point is that the argument from illusion is *inconclusive*, if its claim that we are never directly aware of external objects is regarded as a matter of fact. The point here is not that the original argument needed further premisses to make it valid, for that would show nothing about whether the conclusion was a matter of fact or of language. Rather it is that even when we make the argument watertight by adding these extra premisses they are themselves open to question in a special way. Everything then turns on the special status of these supplementary principles, and Ayer sufficiently indicates their oddity by claiming that they have two characteristics, namely (1) they can be denied without contradiction and (2) they do not appear to admit of any empirical proof.[1]

There is perhaps no general reason to doubt the existence of claims with such special features, but it is worth noting already two points about the argument. First, if what Ayer says about the extra premiss is right, it cannot express a linguistic claim in the sense explained in the previous chapter. For in that sense to deny a necessary linguistic truth would be inconsistent or self-contradictory. If, in Ayer's example, the premiss is true and can be denied without contradiction, then it must be linguistic in some other sense. Second, it might be doubted whether Ayer's strategy in this part of his argument is sound. It is surely inadequate to say that a conclusion is linguistic, on the ground that if it were treated as a matter of fact the argument leading to it would be inconclusive. What such a ground really shows is that the conclusion may be interpreted either as a matter of fact or as a matter of language. What is at issue, then, is not so much whether the conclusion is linguistic and not factual, but only whether it can be interpreted in a linguistic as well as in a factual way.

Ayer does not consider that the crucial extra premiss may be ambiguous, and yet it is not hard to offer quite different accounts of it. The claim, after all, presupposes a distinction between veridical

---

[1] Ayer actually ascribes the second feature only to the first two of his three candidates; but since our premiss is one of these the qualification does not affect the argument. op. cit., p. 12.

and delusive perception, and consequently also a distinction between our perception of objects and the objects themselves. For we might say that the former distinction is that between cases where our perception matches what is really there (veridical perception), and cases where our perception does not match what is really there (delusive perception). But if we accept these contrasts, then the antecedent of the hypothetical premiss may be understood in two radically different ways. In the first it supposes that veridical and delusive perceptions are perceptions of *objects* of different kinds. In the second it supposes that veridical and delusive perceptions are *perceptions* of objects of different kinds.

What could be meant by supposing that veridical and delusive perceptions are perceptions of different kinds of *object*? Importantly the answers to this question depend upon what is to count as an object of the same or a different kind, and the argument offers no help at all in settling that issue. But certainly one natural way to understand the claim would be to paraphrase it as 'There is a difference in the kind of objects we perceive when we perceive veridically and when we perceive delusively'. And, so paraphrased, the claim might be held to be true. When I have a veridical perception of a black saloon car there really is an object of that kind to be the object of my perception. But when I have a delusive perception of a black saloon car there simply is no such thing of that kind to be the object of my perception. So understood the claim expresses a general view about the nature of the difference between veridical and delusive perception, in terms of their different relationships to external objects. But the radical ambiguity over what is to count as an object of the same or a different kind ensures that there are numerous other interpretations of the claim, in some of which it may be false. In the cases just noted, for example, the objects of the veridical and delusive perceptions might have been respectively a black and a dark green saloon car. But it is perfectly open to us to say that these objects are of the same kind, namely both saloon cars.

At least the present interpretation of the antecedent reflects an accepted view of the distinction between veridical and delusive perception, so that the claim comes out true. What the hypothetical premiss asserts as a whole, on this interpretation, is that if there is (as we admit) a difference in the type of object perceived in veridical and delusive perception, then (we should expect that) the perceptions themselves should be qualitatively distinguishable. That is, on the supposition expressed in the antecedent, we should expect to be able to tell from the intrinsic character of the perceptions whether they are veridical or not. Surely, however, it is now obvious that on this supposition we should quite certainly have no such expectations at all. Indeed we might even say that on this interpretation the two parts of the hypothetical premiss are in fundamental conflict. For the first part insists that the essential difference between perceiving veridically and delusively lies *not* in the perceptions themselves, but in their relation to external objects. But the second part asserts that just for that reason we should expect to be able to tell from the perceptions themselves, without considering their relation to external objects, whether they are veridical or not. The consequent appears quite blatantly to assert something which the antecedent has already denied.

That the hypothetical so understood is not a straightforward contradiction can be easily shown. For it might be the case that the contrast between veridical and delusive perception is as we have drawn it in the antecedent, and yet that we were able to tell from the perceptions themselves whether they were veridical or not. It might be the case that although the essential difference between veridical and delusive perception lay in their different relations to external objects, yet we were sufficiently careful and so knowledgeable that we knew all the telltale signs which would enable us to separate veridical from delusive perception 'intrinsically'. In such a position we might gamble on our ability to distinguish them in this way, and always turn out to be right. We would then be in something like the position of art dealers authenticating a picture on internal evidence and amazingly always found to be correct by reference to an independent and decisive test. As things are such a possibility and such expectations run quite counter to our experience, because we are not very careful in our perception and not omniscient either.

In the second interpretation, in which the stress is placed on the *perception* of different kinds of object, the antecedent is false. In this case what the antecedent claims is that the difference between veridical and delusive perception lies only in the *perceptions* of different kinds of object, and not in any relation between perception and external objects. In this case, too, there are innumerable ways of expressing the claim. It might be put by saying that there is some specifiable kind of object perceived always and only in either veridical or delusive perception; or that the essential difference between the two kinds of perception lies in some 'qualitative' difference between them; or that there is some difference in the 'content' of our perceptions which would enable us to distinguish immediately between descriptions of veridical and those of delusive perception. Such claims as these are not, as things are, believed to be true.

The distinction we ordinarily draw between veridical and delusive perception is not a difference between the intrinsic character of the perceptions, though it might be accompanied by some such difference as in the fantasy of omniscience. On this interpretation the antecedent is false, and the hypothetical as a whole is counterfactual. What it asserts is 'If the difference between veridical and delusive perception were a difference in the perceptions themselves (which it is not), then we would expect to be able to tell merely from those perceptions whether they were veridical or not'. Taken in this way the hypothetical is plainly a necessary truth, for the consequent simply follows from the antecedent. If the difference between the two kinds of perception were to be found in the perceptions themselves, then, of course, it would be able to be found in them. As a matter of fact things are not like this; nor is this at all how we normally understand the distinction between veridical and delusive perception.

These two interpretations of the hypothetical premiss have very different characteristics. The first is factually false, but might be true in a world rather unlike our own. The second is a necessary truth, whose denial would be self-contradictory. It seems, therefore, inevitable to suggest that Ayer's initial characterisations of the premiss really belong separately to different versions of it. In the first version since it is factually false it can be denied without contradiction. On the other hand for that reason it clearly is vulnerable to empirical data. The second version by contrast cannot be denied without contradiction, but just for that reason does not appear to admit of, or need, empirical proof. But for the radical ambiguity in its terms, which allows many other interpretations than those so far identified, we might say without qualification that Ayer's characterisation of the premiss is a conflation of properties belonging to quite different premisses.

These ambiguities are sufficiently serious to make the original argument quite inadequate. They also conceal rather than disclose the claimed linguistic character of the extra premiss. On one interpretation the premiss is just empirically false; and on the other, although it is necessarily true, Ayer's use of it clearly involves reference to matters of fact. For Ayer assumes that the consequent of the hypothetical is false, that is, that we cannot as a matter of fact always tell merely from the perceptions themselves whether they are veridical or not. Formally, therefore, he is entitled to deny the antecedent and this may appear to establish just the similarity between veridical and delusive perception which was required to establish the original conclusion. But it is just at this point that the noted ambiguities remain. In at least some plausible interpretations of the antecedent it would still not follow that we are never directly aware of external objects. We might allow, for example, that exactly the same descriptive resources can be used in both veridical and delusive perception, or that there is no difference in the vocabulary we may use in describing veridical and delusive perception, but still say that in the former cases we are directly aware of external objects.[1]

In one way, however, the ambiguities in the premiss are irrelevant to Ayer's argument, for the premiss itself is also irrelevant. The conclusion that he seems to want to reach is in any case directly available either from a consideration of illusions or from the distinction between veridical and delusive perception. Any particular case of illusion, such as that of the 'convergent' railway lines, might lead us to distinguish between phenomenal and objective descriptions of perception. In a phenomenal description what is recorded is the way things appear to the observer without commitment to the way things really are; in objective descriptions there is such a commitment so that it is claimed that particular external objects really exist or have certain features. Such a distinction is required for the contrast between veridical and delusive perception, for the former requires identity and the latter difference between phenomenal and objective descriptions. If we wish to retain an independent sense for the phrase 'direct awareness', then we may still deny that we are directly aware only of phenomenal objects or features. But in Ayer's language this latter claim is a necessary truth, for direct awareness is explicitly confined to such phenomenal objects. This account may usefully remind us that the difference between these descriptions is not one of vocabulary or content. The description of a painting as a 'genuine Vermeer' is not just a description of the observable content of the painting, but we can still employ such terms in a phenomenal description by saying, for example, that what we are seeing looks like a genuine Vermeer. The terms 'looks' and 'appears' sometimes function in this way as indicators of phenomenal descriptions.[2]

---

[1] We might even say, as Austin claimed (op. cit., p. 25), that we may be directly aware of external objects even in cases of illusion, for example where we undoubtedly see a car but mistake its colour. Austin held that it was plausible to deny direct awareness only in cases of total delusion, and that Ayer's use of the term 'delusive' to cover all non-veridical perception was consequently misleading. cf. note to p. 81 above.

[2] cf. C. W. K. Mundle, *Perception: Facts and Theories* (Oxford, 1971), ch. 1. Mundle appears to be making a similar distinction between phenomenal and objective descriptions of perception. But he also distinguishes the former from descriptions of what one is 'perceptually conscious of' (pp. 12–13), and seems to impose vocabulary restrictions on phenomenal descriptions (p. 14).

Ayer's position at this point could be put by saying that he wishes to restrict descriptions of what we perceive to those of a phenomenal kind. Such a restriction, as we have understood it, implies no limitation of the vocabulary used in such descriptions but only one on the commitment made in them. The language Ayer wishes to construct contains perceptual descriptions, all of which are to be understood as neutral or non-committal with respect to the existence and properties of external objects. The term 'sense-datum' is introduced to stand generally for this restriction to the phenomenal objects of perception, and it is in terms of this introduced restriction that Ayer is prepared to accept the additional premiss and the original argument. When Ayer concluded that the objects of veridical and delusive perception were of the same type, he meant only that we might identify such phenomenal objects both in veridical and delusive perception. Whether we are perceiving veridically or delusively we may, if we choose, restrict our perceptual descriptions to those of a neutral, phenomenal, kind. We might have done this even if illusions had not existed, though admittedly in that case it might not have occurred to us to do so.

Understood in this way Ayer's position plainly has many linguistic features, but it also has reference to many facts as well. It involves the introduction of technical terms such as 'sense-data', 'sensing' and 'direct awareness'. It seems natural, though unclear, to regard Ayer as constructing the basis for a new language restricted to phenomenal descriptions. But it was not primarily on these grounds that the issue was held to be linguistic; nor is it linguistic in the sense in which such issues relate to existing languages and their conventions. For Ayer is not concerned to record or unearth the conventions of an existing language such as English, but instead to construct a new technical language for perception. Such a new language may be based on English but will also deviate from the latter in imposing its restriction to phenomenal descriptions. In some ways, therefore, the new conventions belong more obviously to the third sense of 'language' identified in Chapter 4. Ayer's language does not already exist, and its stipulated conventions may deviate from any current usage. It picks out a special subject-matter and defines its technical terms to apply to that restricted area. Its function is, moreover, to formulate a doctrine about perception which, whatever its precise nature, might be called a theory.

In that case, however, it is clear that the position must also involve questions of fact. Merely to invent a new language cannot guarantee a successful application to the facts of perception. If the new language is thought to have achieved this it is presumably because the technical terms are introduced by means of words in current use which themselves relate to familiar facts about perception. Ayer's concluding claim that veridical and delusive perception both have phenomenal objects is a necessary truth in his language, but the phenomenal objects have to be identified through the facts of perception. Ayer's argument, of course, also contained factual premises about the existence of illusions and our inability always to tell from the perceptions themselves whether they are veridical or delusive. We might also say that the constructed language differs from English at least in its initial refusal to acknowledge certain facts, namely those relating to the existence and features of particular external objects. Finally we might expect that the facts of success or failure in achieving the ultimate goals of the construction will be relevant to the acceptability of the language or theory.

These considerations argue that the sharp division between issues of fact and language cannot here be sustained. Linguistic convention and fact inevitably interact in many complex ways. Nevertheless the account also suggests an explanation of Ayer's original characterisation of the extra premiss, on which he based his claim that the issue was linguistic and not factual. We have interpreted Ayer's claim that veridical and delusive perceptions both have phenomenal objects as a necessary truth, based on the conventions introducing the term 'phenomenal object'. Hence that part of the premiss may appear to be unrelated to facts and so to admit of no empirical proof. But the conventions which establish this necessary truth in the new language are themselves not necessary truths, and may be accepted or rejected. The restrictions they embody are not made, for example, in English. Hence it is possible to reject or revise such conventions without inconsistency. These points may make it look as if we have a reference to a single claim which does not admit of empirical proof and yet can be denied without contradiction. But such a conclusion would again involve a conflation of properties belonging to distinct claims, namely the necessary truth and the convention which establishes it. Again, it may seem as though the new conventions make no reference to facts just because, as stipulations, they do not rest on facts of existing usage. But although the premiss is true the conclusion does not follow. The application of the new conventions does depend ultimately upon some connection with the facts of perception; and their acceptability will depend upon the success or failure of the theory of which they form a part.

2. *The second argument for a linguistic reinterpretation*

In Ayer's second argument he goes on to consider, primarily for illustrative purposes, the grounds for accepting the original premiss in the argument from illusion, that we sometimes have perceptual illusions. The problematic part of the argument has usually been regarded as the step from this premiss to the conclusion that we never directly perceive external objects, while the premiss has seemed as a matter of fact incontestable. Ayer now claims that there is no need to accept even this premiss, so long as we are prepared to change our conception of an external object. He shows that our recognition of a conflict in the rival claims of two observers about the shape of an external object, and so our feeling that one of them must be suffering from an illusion, rest on the prior belief that there is just one object in question and not two. Or again our belief that it is a perceptual illusion when the apparent shape of an object changes as we move round it and our angle of vision alters, rests on the assumption that the object is the same, or that it does not change its actual shape. If such assumptions as these were systematically rejected, then the apparent conflicts between perceptual judgments would be resolved, and the grounds for speaking of an illusion would disappear.

Ayer consequently thinks that a man who denies the existence of illusions by rejecting such conventional assumptions could not be refuted empirically. Such a man, by multiplying external objects and making them, in Austin's phrase, 'spryer' than they are normally taken to be, is not open to factual refutation. For his disagreement with our ordinary beliefs is not over rival hypotheses within a common language, but over the choice of alternative languages. Evidently it is Ayer's intention to claim that just as this disagreement is linguistic and not factual, so the whole argument from illusion and the disagreement among philosophers about its conclusion involve a similarly linguistic non-factual dispute.

One initial point about Ayer's argument is that the premiss which now appears as the subject of a linguistic dispute was originally held to be a straightforward matter of fact. Earlier it was noted that a contingent factual claim may nevertheless be the subject of a linguistic disagreement, if for example the disputants disagree about the meanings of its terms. But in such a case we should not infer from the fact that a claim is the subject of a linguistic dispute that the claim itself is linguistic and not factual. In that case within a common language the disagreement can be simply resolved by establishing the sense of the disputed terms in accordance with the conventions of the language. In Ayer's case, however, it is not that the disputants disagree about the meaning of a term in a common language, but that their apparently conflicting claims are made within quite different languages. For one disputant assumes the ordinary conventions governing the terms 'external object' and 'illusion', while the other rejects these in favour of certain new conventions.

In the background of language (1), in which illusions are possible, we ascribe to external objects a stability and independence of observers which allows them to remain the same when our perception of them changes, or when different observers perceive them differently. In the background of language (2) illusions are somehow ruled out by rejecting these assumptions. In language (2) external objects never remain the same when our perception of them alters, or when two observers perceive them differently. A change in, or apparent conflict between, perceptions carries with it a consequential change in the number and properties of external objects. In one language the claim 'We never have perceptual illusions' is factually false, but in the other it seems to have acquired the status of a linguistic truth. Apparently the status of such a claim may vary with the linguistic background in which it is made.

The details of such differences of language are still blurred. We have a sketch-map of the proposed new language rather than a detailed blueprint. It is not clear, for example, whether the term 'external object' in the new language is just equivalent to 'perception' in the old. Nor is it clear whether in the new language such a claim as 'Jones has just had a perceptual illusion' cannot be expressed, is necessarily false, or even simply untestable. It is possible that language (2) might be constructed to admit the idea of an illusion as meaningful, and yet to contain no way of determining when illusions took place. A speaker of such a language would then be in something like the position of traditional philosophers who admitted the possibility of things in themselves but declared them to be unknowable.

But whatever the details of such a new language may be, it is natural to describe one difference between it and the alternative by saying that while the former does not officially recognise a range of facts about illusions, the latter does. Whether in language (2) we say that a claim about someone's having a perceptual illusion cannot be made, is false, or is empty at least the language officially withholds recognition from a class of facts which are recognised in the alternative system. It would no doubt be quite wrong to think

of such languages as bringing illusions or external objects into
existence, or thrusting them out of it. Just as a man who refuses to
admit the category 'disease' is not carrying out a programme of
preventive medicine, so language (2) is not, except in a bizarre way,
ensuring that our perception never goes wrong. Nevertheless in its
imposed restrictions and its deviation from the alternative language
the new system undoubtedly offers a new way of looking at reality.
Within the framework of language (2) a whole area of experience
admitted in the alternative system goes unrecorded and unrecognised.

In the light of such claims it is puzzling to find Ayer insisting
throughout the argument that in general, and in this particular case,
alternative languages express exactly the same facts. He says, for
example,

In the case of sense-data it is a question of there being extraneous grounds
for preferring one method of description to another, which is equally true
to the facts (op. cit., p. 28).

And in relation to the particular dispute over illusions he says

Where we say that two observers are seeing the same material thing, he
prefers to say that they are seeing different things which, however, have
some structural properties in common. But the facts to which these
expressions are intended to refer are in either case the same (op. cit.,
p. 18).

Evidently it is required that Ayer should hold some such view so long
as he wishes to characterise the difference between the disputants
in all these cases as linguistic and not factual.

Apart from the general thesis that linguistic change is in any case
empty and makes therefore no difference to the facts, there are two
particular ways in which such a view might be defended. But neither
is at all satisfactory. In the first it is claimed that the only facts to be
identified in the dispute are those which can be recognised by both
languages. Certainly there is some temptation to take this view,
since these facts form a kind of common denominator to both
systems and are presumably agreed between the disputants. But it
would be obviously wrong to accept as a general principle that what
counts as a fact in some dispute is just what the disputants are
agreed about. If we wish to draw a distinction between factual and
linguistic considerations at all, then we should allow for the possi-
bilities of agreement and disagreement over both. To accept the
general principle would be to turn every dispute into one of language.

It might, however, be said that what counts as a fact is relative to a particular language. But from this we should not draw the conclusion that in such disagreements there is no dispute over facts, but rather that in such cases there is no way of telling whether there is factual disagreement or not. Further we might also draw the conclusion that such disputes between languages are factual disputes as well, that is, are disputes over what is to count as a fact.

The second way would be to assume that the two alternative languages are in the end equivalent, so that every claim made in one can in principle be translated into the other. But such a move is open to two quite decisive objections. First, although Ayer undoubtedly wished to say that his sense-datum language and the material object language are equivalent, he could not be justified in *assuming* such an equivalence at this stage of the argument. The new language in this case was set up precisely to see whether such a goal could be attained. The success of the construction cannot be taken for granted in characterising the nature of the construction itself. This difficulty also applies to the illustrative case about illusions, but here a further objection arises. For in this case there is no suggestion that the two languages are equivalent. On the contrary in order to maintain some difference between the disputants it seemed to be presupposed that the equivalence did not obtain.

These points indicate a serious qualification to be made to the claim that the disagreements in Ayer's examples are linguistic and not factual. We might say that the standard factual disagreement is one which occurs within a common agreed language. The disputants know and agree about the meaning of the disputed claim, but they disagree about whether the claim is contingently true or false. Hence the disagreement in both of Ayer's examples is not a standard factual disagreement, for the disputants in these cases do not share and agree about a common language. But it would surely be wrong to infer from this that the dispute is not about facts at all. For one thing the strict inference could be only that the disagreement is not of a *standard* factual kind. But it is also plain that there is room for a characterisation of the dispute in terms of facts. We may say, for example, that it is a dispute over what is to count as a fact, or whether to recognise officially a certain range of facts. It is true that this reference to facts is achieved, or avoided, precisely by means of certain linguistic conventions. But this may lead us to say that the dispute is both linguistic and factual, rather than that it is linguistic but not factual.

Equally, the kind of argument used to show that these disagree-

ments are not of a standard factual kind may be used to show that
they are not of a standard linguistic sort either. We might say that
the standard linguistic disagreement is one which occurs precisely
about the meaning of a term in some particular language common
to the disputants. You think that in English 'deciduous' means 'not
bearing cones', and I think it means 'shedding leaves in the autumn'.
But in Ayer's cases the disagreement plainly is not of this sort,
since it is assumed that the disputants are employing distinct alternative languages. Hence in these cases just as the issue is not of a
standard factual kind, so it is not of a standard linguistic sort. If
there is disagreement at all, then it is not disagreement about what
the meaning of a term is in some given language, but about which
of its meanings in two different languages is to be preferred. But if
this is so, then in the area of such non-standard disputes there seems
no merit in making an exclusive choice between saying that the
dispute is linguistic or is factual. There is as good ground for saying
that such disputes are neither linguistic nor factual as for saying that
they are both linguistic and factual. What seems wrong is to describe
such disputes as linguistic but not factual at all, that is, to suppose
that the application of one of the terms must exclude the other.

Despite these difficulties in Ayer's position his argument brings
out, what might otherwise have gone unnoticed, that our beliefs
about illusions rest upon certain background conventions or
principles. These conventions may be represented as part of a
language, but they are not sacrosanct and may be revised or rejected
in favour of others. It is a merit in Ayer's account that the existence
and special status of these background principles should be disclosed
but it is not a merit unique to Ayer. Traditional philosophers also
had unearthed similar principles and noted their peculiarities. Kant,
for example, described certain background principles as 'conditions
of the possibility of experience', and both Hume and Russell identified
certain others as 'instinctive beliefs'. These terminologies for describing the special status of such principles, like Ayer's characterisation of them as 'linguistic', were a conscious attempt to capture
something of their admitted peculiarity.

Nevertheless although traditional philosophers had noted the
existence of such principles there is one important respect in which
their accounts generally differed from Ayer's. For while earlier
philosophers usually stressed the inviolability or necessity of such
principles Ayer wished to stress their vulnerability to change, and
even to recommend changes in them. It may be that some such
principles are genuinely inviolable, and even that arbitrary proposals

to change others cannot be justified, but it can scarcely be doubted that some of them are open to revision. There may be theoretical or practical benefits to be obtained by changes in the sense, or in criteria for the application, of terms. No doubt Ayer's account should be supplemented by an account of the conditions in which such revisions may be justified, but it is natural to say that proposals which confer no benefits and are motivated simply by the desire to win an argument stand a good chance of being unjustified. Even by this meagre standard Ayer's two proposals are very different. For while he stresses the consequential tests for his genuine proposal about the introduction of the term 'sense-datum', in the other illustrative case similar points are not made. In the latter case the proposed change is motivated apparently by the desire to win the argument, and there is no suggestion of any beneficial consequences to follow. Certainly the apparent advantage of eliminating illusions is itself quite illusory. Consequently we might regard these proposals as arbitrary or empty, but if so then this is not because any such change in language is empty, but because in this case a condition of the legitimate exercise of the privilege has been violated. That such violations may occur, or that some proposals are illegitimate, is an indication that linguistic change as such cannot be regarded as empty.

Ayer's description of the background conventions as linguistic consequently has some value. Not only does it serve to pick out the function of such conventions in relation to our experience, but it also stresses that these conventions are in principle revisable. But there remains still a radical ambiguity over what is to count as a language. In his original argument Ayer wished to draw a sharp distinction between rival hypotheses within a common language and alternative languages. But it was suggested earlier that in some respects Ayer's alternative system seemed more like a theory than a language. Although still expressed in English it appears to be a deviation from that language, and may best be understood as a conscious restriction to part of the language for some technical purpose. In this way the new system looks like some technical theory branching off from our ordinary non-technical terminology. Indeed Ayer himself subsequently used the term 'theory' in this context when he claimed that 'our conception of the physical world can be exhibited as a theory with respect to our experiences'.[1] If our ordinary conventions relating to physical or external objects are taken to represent or be part of a theory, then presumably the rival conven-

[1] A. J. Ayer, *The Origins of Pragmatism* (London, 1968), p. 303.

tions in the alternative systems should have the same status. Yet it is still not clear how, if at all, we should distinguish between the conventions of a language and the principles of a theory.

For all these reasons it is difficult to attach any decisive or final merit to Ayer's own account. Perhaps the description of the background conventions as linguistic has some contribution to make to an understanding of their function and status. But what has so far been said suggests that such a description is at least as misleading or incomplete as it is correct. It is misleading, for example, in so far as it suggests an exclusive division between language and fact. It is misleading in so far as it suggests that there is no place for a reference to facts in disputes of the kind Ayer regards as linguistic. And it is misleading in its suggestion that linguistic change is empty, or neutral with respect to facts. It seemed to offer a final explanation of certain background conventions as belonging to language. Instead it points to the further task of clarifying the nature and range of these conventions, and the ideas of a language and theory associated with them.

6

SCEPTICISM

The sceptic stalks prominently through recent philosophical literature. Certainly no historical figure has ever matched the ingenuity or complexity with which the sceptic has been credited, but that is no reason to disregard his problems. Indeed some philosophers have managed to suggest that scepticism is the central issue in philosophy, although others have regarded such issues as futile or empty.[1] It is quite common to find complaints from non-philosophers about the spurious nature of philosophical problems directed to these sceptical arguments. But in one way these complaints are less than fair to the current interest in the topic; for most recent philosophers have been concerned with scepticism in order to refute the doctrine and not to indulge in it. In this chapter something will be said of the nature and complexity of the issue, in order to separate what, if anything, is of value in the arguments from what is useless in them.

1. *Standard scepticism and its varieties*

Sceptical arguments certainly take many different forms, but it is helpful at least to begin by presenting what may be called a standard scepticism, so that variations in the sceptic's position can be measured against this standard. Such a standard scepticism may be illustrated by reference to the traditional doubts about our knowledge of external objects. Such doubts might arise from the argument from illusion, but it is not necessary to appeal to that device. Instead it may simply be noted that we base claims about the properties of

[1] J. Wisdom in *Philosophy and Psycho-Analysis* and R. W. Newell in *The Concept of Philosophy* (London, 1967) attach great importance to sceptical issues. J. Locke in his *Essay Concerning Human Understanding*, Book I, ch. 1, § 5, and J. L. Austin in *Philosophical Papers* (Oxford, 1961) dismiss them.

D

external objects upon our sensory experience. We ascribe a colour, shape, or structure to an object on the basis of the way it looks, or feels, or sounds to us. Put more linguistically we base claims of the form 'That ball is red', or 'That coin is round', or 'That tree is hollow' on such claims as 'It looks red', 'It looks (feels) round', and 'It looks (feels, sounds) hollow'. But the relation between these two sets of claims, or two languages, which we have expressed by means of the phrase 'is based upon' is not wholly clear. It is natural to assume that if such a relation is to be justified at all, then it must be justified either deductively or inductively. But the attempt to justify the step from the claims in the basis to the others, either deductively or inductively, seems doomed to failure.

For the relation seems not to be simply deductive. There is no contradiction in saying, for example, 'That sounds hollow, but it is in fact solid', or 'It looks pinkish in this light, but it is actually yellow'. It may seem more hopeful to look for an inductive justification, in which the way things look, or feel, or sound to us is taken as empirical evidence of the way things actually are. But at this point there appears to be a decisive objection to such an attempt. For if the relation is to be justified in this way then it must rest on some observed correlation between the way things look and their actual properties. But to make any such correlation would be to assume just what the sceptic is already doubting, namely that we can justify claims about the actual properties on the basis of the way things look, or feel, or sound to us. Any such attempt to provide an inductive justification will be circular, at least so long as there is no independent way of establishing the properties of external objects. Such an attempt simply begs the question whether we are entitled to base claims about the properties of external objects on our sensory experiences.

A similar argument was developed in Hume's attack on induction itself. Our claims about the future are naturally based upon an experience of associations in the past. In the past winter months have been invariably followed by the summer months and these in turn by winter. We come to expect with complete confidence that the same sequence will persist in the future. But the relation between these sets of claims is not wholly clear. As Hume said (*Inquiry*, Book I, Section IV, Part II), 'I shall allow if you please that one proposition may be inferred from the other: I know in fact that it always is inferred. But if you insist that the inference is made by a chain of reasoning, I desire you to produce that reasoning'. For the relation between a claim about past regularities, even if invariable, and a prediction about the future is not simply deductive. There is no contradiction in saying that although bread has nourished me in the past it may not do so in the future. But an inductive justification for the relation seems even less promising, since it is precisely induction which is at issue. To appeal to inductive procedures to justify induction seems blatantly circular.

Hume has another way of putting the point. A justification might be found if we could establish a general principle of induction, formulated perhaps as 'The future resembles the past', or 'Nature is uniform'. For such a principle might enable us, in conjunction with a claim about past resemblance or past uniformity, to deduce a future occurrence. Perhaps a similar hope might be entertained for a general principle of resemblance between the way things look and their actual properties, in the case of scepticism about external objects. But the value of appealing to such principles is very dubious. They do not seem to be necessary truths, since they can be denied without contradiction. But if they are contingent truths which require to be supported by inductive correlations, then such support again involves the original circularity. Hume's conclusion was that these principles, and the procedures they represent, lack a rational justification and can be regarded only as reflecting an instinctive, mechanical habit which is, luckily, unavoidable.

In these examples the central features of standard scepticism can be easily picked out. First, two kinds of claim must be identified, one of which is taken as the natural basis for asserting the other. Second, it is assumed that if this relation between the two kinds of claim is to be justified, then the justification must be either deductive or inductive. Third, it is argued that the relation between the claims is not simply deductive; and fourth, it is argued that an inductive justification would be circular. It should be added that the argument is used sceptically only where the conclusion expresses some doubt about the problematic claims.

Once such a standard argument is identified there is no difficulty in multiplying instances of the same pattern. Examples well known in philosophy arise from the relation between claims about a man's behaviour and claims about his mental state; or from the relation between claims about similarity and claims about identity. Once again the relation between the claims in each of these cases is not that of simple deduction, and yet any inductive support for the step from one to the other presupposes the establishment of the claims which are themselves at issue in the argument. But there is no reason so far to restrict the range of scepticism to the philosophically

familiar examples. A less familiar example might be constructed
on the supposition that a physicist might attempt to measure a remote
star's temperature on the basis of its spectrum. The physicist might
argue that since there is a well-established correlation between
spectra and temperature in observed terrestrial cases he is entitled
to infer temperature from an analysis of the spectrum even in non-
terrestrial cases. But now the requirements for a sceptical argument
seem to be satisfied. There are two kinds of claim, or two languages,
about spectra and about temperature; and the former claims are
in this case the basis for asserting the latter. But the step from spectrum to temperature is not simply deductive, since there is no
contradiction in denying the supposed correlation. And any inductive attempt seems to presuppose just what is at issue, namely that
we can in the disputed case empirically correlate spectra and temperature.

So far the sceptic has been given an artificially unified appearance,
but his arguments may vary considerably from the standard in
many different kinds of way. One variation might arise from apparent
differences in the availability of an independent or direct access to
the disputed items. A sceptic may insist less on the circularity of any
attempt at inductive justification than on the impossibility of such
an independent access. There may seem, for this reason, to be a
significant difference in the topics to which the sceptic's arguments
are directed. It may be said, for example, that independent, though
not perhaps direct, access to the temperature of a remote star is
technically but not logically impossible; while such independent or
direct access to another person's mental state is logically rather than
technically impossible. But in none of these cases is it even faintly
clear what would count as independent or direct access, and in the
absence of such clarity variations of this sort are impossible to assess.

A more decisive set of variants arises generally from differences
in the conclusions drawn from the standard argument. Even in
traditional philosophy it was common to distinguish sceptics in
terms of the strength of their doubt. Kant, for example, distinguishes
the dogmatic from the problematic idealist, where the latter regards
the existence of external objects as only doubtful and the former
regards it as impossible (*Critique of Pure Reason*, B 274). Similarly
Hume, in his sophisticated catalogue of sceptical variants in the
Inquiry (Book I, Section XII), separates what he calls an 'excessive'
from a 'mitigated' doubt. But these variations in the topic or strength
of the doubt are less interesting than those in the scope or object
of the doubt.

It is, for example, quite usual for philosophers to illustrate a sceptical position by reference to quite particular claims of the kind at issue. Thus we are sometimes invited to consider how we could justify the claim that a man on a particular occasion has a certain mental state on the basis of our observation of his present behaviour. Yet it is sometimes said that philosophical scepticism characteristically applies doubt rather to whole classes of claim than to particular members of the class. But this apparent division between a general and a particular sceptic conceals some ambiguity. For it is not clear what is the relation between a general doubt applied to a class of claims and a particular doubt applied to members of that class. In one way it seems that to doubt a class of claims would be to doubt each member of the class. Yet it is plain that the sceptic's attitude to specific cases is quite unlike that in which we may express doubt about them in everyday life. Everyday doubts occur in a context in which generally we have a perfect understanding of what would relieve those doubts. I may wonder whether on this occasion I locked the front door because I cannot now remember doing so, but when the relevant memory is vivid and distinct then I have no such doubts at all. The sceptic is not concerned in his argument to differentiate between such everyday doubts and certainties; if he were, then he would be forced to admit that at least on some occasions there is no room for doubt. For his purposes all cases, whether classed as certain or not by everyday standards, are in some way equally doubtful.

Hence the distinction between a general and a particular sceptic conceals a different contrast between what may be called theoretical and practical doubt. The sceptic's doubt is not of the practical kind faced in everyday life. It rests instead on a quite general argument which treats all particular cases in the same way, whether in everyday life they would be regarded as doubtful or not. The sceptic's doubt is consequently theoretical rather than practical, and it is in this special way that he questions classes of claims and particular members of those classes. It is partly for this reason that the sceptic's questioning seems to be quite distinct and insulated from practical considerations. And it is for this reason that sceptics like Descartes and Hume have nevertheless not behaved in everyday life as if there were any practical doubt about particular cases. It is quite consistent to doubt a whole class of cases in this theoretical way, and still behave as if the particular claims, or some general principle underlying them, were true. Such a sceptic may all the same express doubt about the particular cases, just as a man who, in Körner's example, adopts the policy of driving as if all other drivers were drunk may nevertheless doubt whether all of them are. The sceptic's kind of doubt is not about particular cases within an accepted framework of reasons and evidence; it is rather about that conventional framework itself.

This is made still more clear in a linguistic variant of the sceptic's conclusion. It might be said on the basis of the standard argument that when we employ a disputed terminology to refer, for example, to external objects, other minds, or the temperature of a remote star we are confused or mistaken about what these terms mean. A sceptic about other minds might put his doubt by saying that claims about another person's mental state are only claims about that person's pattern of behaviour. In the spectrum-temperature case it may be said that a claim about the temperature of a remote star means nothing more than that the star has a certain spectrum. Such moves are typically associated with positivist or operationalist doctrines about meaning. The suggestion is that in ordinary life we accept the disputed terms at face value because we assume certain fictions, which the standard sceptical argument shows to be unwarranted. These fictions in the guise of general principles, like the principle of induction, form part of a framework which misleads us into attaching a spurious sense to the disputed terms. What the sceptic suggests is that these fictions should be eliminated from scientific discourse by removing the spurious elements from the meaning of the disputed terms. What the sceptic offers is a change in the framework that we ordinarily accept. Final certainty is achieved, but at the cost of conceding the doubtfulness of the claims in their conventional interpretation.

2. *Varieties of refutation*

Just as the sceptic's positions offer a complex variety of view, so it is to be expected that attempts at a refutation of the sceptic will be equally complex. Indeed it seems reasonable to think that part of the sceptic's power lies less in the soundness of his argument than in the elusiveness of his conclusions. It is scarcely to be expected that there is just one refutation of the sceptic, any more than there is just one treatment for a family of diseases. By the same token we should not think a refutation has failed merely because the sceptic has other positions to retreat to; nor should we think that a treatment suitable for one topic will be equally suitable for all. Any particular attempt at a refutation may have a specific function in eliminating one version of the doctrine in its application to one topic. We shall find that

most of the attempts considered here have some value, but that
neither singly nor together are they sufficient to refute the sceptic
once and for all.

Some attempts at refutation have concentrated on formal weak-
nesses in the standard argument, and two of these should be noted
here without further discussion. In the first of these the claimed
weak point in the standard argument is its assumption that the
relation between claims in the basis and disputed claims must be
justified either deductively or inductively. If such an assumption
were false, and induction and deduction did not exhaust the range of
possible justifications, then there would be at least the possibility
of giving some alternative account of the questionable relation.
Some philosophers have wanted to offer such an alternative account,
and have consequently ascribed the persistence of sceptical arguments to a mistaken and narrow belief that induction and deduction
together exhaust the range of possible justification.[1] These alternative
relations have been variously described by saying that the claims in
the basis provide criteria for the application of the disputed terms,
or that the former give an *a priori* reason, which is neither inductive
nor deductive, for accepting the disputed claims. It is suggested
that although the claim 'It is hollow' cannot be deduced from 'It
sounds hollow', nevertheless the complex claim 'There is a reason for
saying that it is hollow' can be deduced from the latter. The view
might be summarised by saying that while the relation is not deductive, the claims in the basis in some way define a set of reasons for
accepting the disputed claims.

The target of the second attempt at refutation is an even more
obvious formal defect in the original argument. For the standard
sceptic was represented as arguing that there can be no deductive
relation between the two sets of claims from the premiss that
there is no simple deductive relation between particular claims
in the basis and the corresponding disputed claim. But it is clear
that such an argument is invalid. For even if it is true that the claim
'It is red' cannot be deduced from the particular claim 'It looks
red', it does not follow that the former cannot be deduced from any
set of basic claims, however complex. What has been admitted in
the premiss is that in one kind of case the deductive relation does
not hold, but nothing has been done to show that it cannot hold in
other kinds of case. Such an argument leaves open the possibility

[1] R. W. Newell, op. cit., *passim*. See also W. Gregory Lycan, 'Non-inductive
Evidence', *American Philosophical Quarterly*, April 1971, for a summary, and
extensive bibliography, of these views.

of demonstrating a deductive relation provided that the claims in
the basis are sufficiently complex and syntactically rich. An ambition
of this reductive kind lay behind Ayer's original introduction of the
sense-datum language. If it could be shown that any claim about
external objects can be translated without remainder into one about
sense-data, then this would refute the relevant scepticism about
external objects. For such a demonstration would reveal that the
relation between the two sets of claims is deductive after all.

In one way these two attempts divide the field between them.
For in answering the sceptic we have the alternatives of either
demonstrating a deductive relation between the claims, or else
assuming certain constitutive principles which recognise the basic
claims as reasons for holding the others. But even though other
attempts at refutation may in the end fall into one or other of these
two positions, they also often throw their own distinctive light on the
sceptic's position. Of these other attempts two will be briefly considered. In the first an appeal to common sense is used to resist the
sceptic, and in the second it is claimed that the sceptic's doubt is in
some way inappropriate or empty.

It has been common both inside and outside philosophy to rely
on common sense to refute scepticism. Dr Johnson's reported
refutation of Berkeley was shorter and less philosophical than
G. E. Moore's defence of common sense or his proof of an external
world. But the same insistence on our ordinary convictions about
particular cases is present in both. In more recent philosophy the
appeal to ordinary language and the paradigm case argument have
continued this tradition of insistence on particular cases and our
ordinary beliefs about them. It is true that these more recent arguments have tried to support our ordinary beliefs with a general
doctrine about language, but it is still our ordinary beliefs about
particular cases which are taken as the target for the sceptic's
attack.

But such arguments against the sceptic are severely limited. They
seem either to establish too little, or else to be over-ambitious. If,
for example, such arguments depend ultimately upon the strength
of our beliefs about particular cases, then the sceptic will naturally
reply that he has no wish to dispute the existence of that conviction.
What concerns him is not so much that we have such a strength of
conviction in these cases, but what the ground for it can be. Merely
to insist on our ordinary beliefs is not so much to defend common
sense as simply to reiterate it. Moreover it was pointed out already
that the sceptic's attitude to particular cases is not the same as the

doubt or hesitation we feel in everyday life. The sceptic would not wish to deny that ordinarily we draw a distinction between particular cases which are doubtful and those which are not, but as far as his argument goes all these cases are equally in need of a justification. The common-sense appeal to particular cases cannot by itself offer any such justification. It may make clear that the sceptic's target is the general framework of our belief rather than the particular cases, but once this is clear the appeal to common sense seems irrelevant.

On the other side the more developed arguments to show not merely that we have such convictions but that somehow our language guarantees their correctness seem far too ambitious. The fact that a term is used consistently to differentiate between the cases to which it applies and those to which it does not apply may show that the term has some meaning in the language. But even if a disputed term is undeniably used to mark some distinction it does not follow that the distinction is exactly what our common-sense convictions believe it to be. A physicist may consistently use temperature terms in the case of remote stars to mark distinctions between spectra. His linguistic activities seem to be rather a pre-condition of the sceptical problem's arising, than a relevant consideration in resolving the problem. Such arguments might have some force when applied to simple ostensive terms, such as colour words, but the sceptic's attacks are generally directed at highly complex terms such as 'temperature', 'external object', or 'identity'. It is generally a mistake to infer directly from the existence of a term in a language to that of some corresponding item in the world. Arguments which rely generally upon some such linguistic guarantee are simply fallacious.

In the next attempt at refutation the argument rightly moves from a common-sense consideration of particular cases to a theoretical account of general issues. In this attempt it is argued that in several ways the sceptic's doubts are inappropriate, unreal, or empty. In one case already considered (p. 71) a sceptic might deny us knowledge of external objects on the ground that claims about such objects are only contingently and not necessarily true. To take such a view would be to demand a standard for knowledge which is clearly inappropriate to contingent claims. Nevertheless it is open to a sceptic, or anyone else, to legislate arbitrarily that the term 'know' should be restricted to such necessary truths. But in this kind of case, as Wisdom pointed out, the force of the legislation is only to point to well-known differences between contingent and necessary truths. These differences may be accepted, however, without further marking them by the restriction on the word 'know' and without drawing any sceptical conclusions. The recommendation is consequently unnecessary, but more than this it seems also to be quite empty. For there is nothing that could conceivably be done to relieve such a doubt. There is no possibility of improving a contingent truth by acquiring further evidence in its favour so that it becomes necessary. Consequently the notion of doubt seems to have no substantial place in the argument.

Wisdom's case has little reference to the standard sceptical argument, but there are similar kinds of case relating to it. The standard argument carries conviction only where there is no independent way of gaining access to the disputed items. If it were possible to gain such independent access, then there would be some independent check on the criterion disputed by the sceptic. It was pointed out earlier that there is nevertheless great unclarity over what is to count as an independent or direct check of the required kind. It might seem obvious, for example, that in the spectrum-temperature case there may well be additional tests which have a bearing on the use of this criterion. It may be found that other tests cohere reasonably well with the spectrum measurement, or even that the assigned temperatures fit in well with other aspects of stellar physics. Considerations of these kinds would be a natural resource for the physicist, but it is always possible for the sceptic to dismiss them. After all they provide no more than indirect or circumstantial support for the assigned temperatures; they do not, any more than the spectrum test does, provide a direct access to the phenomenon. Hence it is always possible for a sceptic simply to legislate against any such extra support for the disputed criterion.

The position in this particular case is, however, no different from that in the others. We may, in a similar way, obtain various kinds of surrounding confirmation which fit well into a unified picture of a man's mental state, or of the properties of external objects, or of the numerical identity of some object. Yet in all these cases a sceptic may simply dismiss any such cross check by legislating against it. It is not so much that in some typically philosophical cases there is a problem about independent access which does not arise in other examples. Rather it is that a sceptic may choose in any example to make his position secure by legislating against any such independent information. But a sceptic who adopts this line secures his position at the expense of making it trivial. Such a position is distinct from the empty recommendation about the word 'know', but its upshot is much the same. We might reasonably say in such cases that the sceptic is canvassing an unreal or empty doubt by legislating that nothing whatever could relieve it.

Finally in this catalogue of unrealities we may note one further case where doubt about a general principle, or criterion, or set of claims, is empty. It has been suggested that some principles required to validate the disputed criteria, and with them a whole area of discourse or enquiry, are strictly indubitable or incorrigible. We may, for example, think of a principle of non-contradiction as generally forbidding the occurrence in any area of enquiry of a proposition and its negation. If so, then it seems impossible seriously to doubt or question such a principle, and impossible to think of devising any rational framework of enquiry which abandoned such a principle. If it could be shown in other cases relating to the sceptic's doubt that the principles or criteria in question were similarly incorrigible and unrevisable, then the doubt in those cases would also be unreal and empty.

In these attempts at refutation we can see the isolation of a class of cases where sceptical doubt is worthless or empty. A sceptic who treats his doubt as exactly parallel to our everyday hesitations may be refuted by a blunt appeal to common sense. One who legislates emptily about the notions of knowledge or of direct and independent tests may also be led to see the futility of his position. And one who raises doubts about a principle which cannot be revised is similarly vulnerable to the charge that his questioning is empty. Such cases may lead us to think that the sceptic has been finally tamed, by removing any genuine doubt from his conclusions. His function could then simply be to describe features of our experience, or to draw attention, as Wisdom said, to similarities and differences between items in it, rather than seriously to revise or doubt those features. Certainly one value which the issue has is to draw attention to the existence and function of constitutive principles in some area of enquiry, and to the way in which these relate to criteria and reasons for asserting the disputed claims. But nothing has been done yet to show that the notion of doubt has been totally eradicated. On the contrary the list of empty doubts points to other cases where the doubt is genuine and substantive.

There are, for example, considerable difficulties in showing that any principle is strictly incorrigible in the required way. Recently a distinction has been drawn between internal and external incorrigibility with respect to the principles of a categorial framework.[1] A principle is internally incorrigible so long as it is an essential part

[1] S. Körner, *Categorial Frameworks*, ch. II.

of its framework, but externally incorrigible only if it is an essential part of any framework. It might still seem that a principle of non-contradiction is bound to satisfy the test for being externally incorrigible, but Körner argues against this. Other principles, such as that linking spectra and temperature in stellar physics, are not externally incorrigible whatever their internal status may be. It is external incorrigibility which is required to show that the sceptic's doubts are empty in a strong sense, but it is by no means easy to tell when a principle has this character. From inside an accepted framework all its essential principles may seem inviolable. Human beings tend to err on the side of intellectual conservatism, and to treat their internally incorrigible principles as though they were externally incorrigible also. It may be psychologically impossible for a historian to question any of the fundamental principles with which he approaches the past, even though these principles are revisable. Or again it may be strictly impossible for a historian to overcome all his local limitations, and yet it is the revolutionary historians in any age who manage to revise or question some of them. In these cases the sceptic's doubt may be directed not emptily at an externally incorrigible principle but at an internally incorrigible fiction.

It may be argued that even if the sceptic's doubt is genuine in this way still his questioning may be empty if he has no particular candidates with which to replace the revisable principles. We might put the point in another way. The general principles so far unearthed stand only as token figureheads for the more specific criteria, procedures, and claims, accepted within some framework. They are far too general to play any substantive role in the operation of the system itself. It is for this reason that they may be regarded as principles standing outside the framework itself but constitutive of it, as conditions of the possibility of a certain area of discourse or enquiry. They mark the mere possibility of using a certain criterion rather than the specific detail of its actual use. A principle of induction, for example, expresses quite generally the acceptance of a procedure in which future events are predicted on the basis of past regularities. But it has by itself no power to tell us more specifically how or when such predictions should or should not be made. No doubt the future does resemble the past, but our specific interest is in learning the respects in which it does so, and the weight to be attached to particular degrees of resemblance. Past regularities, for example, often provide only a probability of some future occurrence, so that further principles are needed to justify firm predictions based on the assessment of probabilities. But it is often a matter of controversy to decide upon the formulation of such specific principles of acceptance.[1] A sceptic, in drawing attention to the status of the fundamental principle, may also wish to question the adequacy of the principles subordinate to it. He may wish not to abandon the general principle but only to modify or refine it so that more adequate subsidiary principles can be found. In this way the sceptic's doubt may be traced from the general principle itself to the further principles which function in the detailed operation of the disputed criteria. Because the specific principles are refinements of the general principle and because they may be genuinely doubtful or unclear the sceptic's doubt may in these cases be treated as legitimate.

Again it is not necessarily an empty speculation to question whether one set of claims may be reduced to another, or whether additional postulates are required to make the connection. It would be satisfyingly economical and theoretically valuable to be able to show that with certain resources from physics it is possible to deduce claims about temperature from descriptions of spectra. It is not a purely idle or empty matter to attempt to reduce number theory to the theory of sets, or to show how set theory itself may be established on the basis of certain logical calculi. And although Ayer subsequently abandoned his claim that propositions about external objects can be reduced to propositions about sense-data, it is not an empty or idle matter to consider what would be required to establish the former on the basis of the latter.[2] Such work may not have any practical implications in confirming our common-sense convictions about the existence and properties of external objects, but it may tell us something of the theoretical framework in which we speak about such objects. Since any such construction would offer a theoretical account of a way in which the language of external objects is based upon sense experiences, it may even provide guidance about the way in which we learn such a language.

In all these ways scepticism cannot be regarded as empty or spurious. Perhaps it is partly for this reason that the issue is so persistent. Not only are the problems intellectually puzzling and sometimes logically irresoluble, but they are also on occasion genuine and valuable. There is, however, a tendency to regard the

[1] See, for example, R. Carnap, *Logical Foundations of Probability* (Chicago, 1950), ch. IV; C. Hempel, *Aspects of Scientific Explanation* (New York, 1965); and D. E. Morrison and R. E. Henkel (Eds.), *The Significance Test Controversy* (London, 1970).
[2] See Nelson Goodman, *The Structure of Appearance* (Harvard, 1951).

genuine doubts about specific principles as non-philosophical, since they are directed more obviously to the working principles of particular disciplines or practices. In this way to refer to philosophical scepticism may be misleadingly to refer only to sceptical issues which are empty or spurious. But the genuine issues that arise out of scepticism may be regarded as in part philosophical. Problems about probable inference and principles of acceptance are not demands for simple empirical observation or enquiry. They involve instead inevitably the understanding of the general notion of probability and the way in which it can be employed in inductive arguments.

Such issues are typical of the background problems which may concern philosophy as well as some particular discipline or practice. It would be futile to debate whether the work of Whitehead and Russell belongs properly to mathematics or philosophy. If a systematic construction of a language for external objects may be employed in theories about the learning of such a language it would be equally pointless to allocate it exclusively to philosophy or psychology. To draw exclusive divisions of these kinds would be to return to the unjustified views rejected in earlier chapters. For the practitioners of some discipline working within an accepted framework it may be difficult to see clearly enough to break out of it. Normal science and normal practice, in Kuhn's sense, are the rule rather than the exception. It is the revolutionary departures from normality which involve revising the accepted principles. It has traditionally been regarded as a standard part of philosophy to encourage such changes, to question or criticise local assumptions, and to recommend or devise alternatives to them. Such an activity is not always valuable; it may be empty or spurious. But it is this task, which may be both genuine and valuable, to which the sceptic's arguments unclearly point.

3. *The languages of chess*

The summary conclusions of the previous section were certainly very general. They may carry more conviction if they can be briefly illustrated in some semi-technical area such as that of chess, which most people may understand. In earlier chapters reference has been made to the language of chess as though this were a single unified technical system. Certainly the phenomenon may be treated in this way, but the situation is more complex than this unity suggests. For we may separate the language required to institute the game of chess from the language devised to guide best play in the game.

In sketching these languages and their relationship we may begin to show something of the complexities involved in talking of languages or theories, and also to throw some illustrative light on the earlier sceptical issues.

When people talk about the language of chess they usually have in mind the rules which are required to institute the game. These rules define such things as the playing area, the pieces, moves, the initial position, and the formal criteria for terminating games. Such a language enables us to record positions or whole games unambiguously, and also to vet moves and positions for illegalities. It may be called the basic chess language (BCL). It is clearly contrasted with, though related to, another language which we may devise for strategic purposes to guide play over the board. Such a strategic chess language (SCL) could be treated along with BCL as part of a unified chess language, but its apparatus and function are quite distinct from those of BCL. SCL will contain methods of evaluating the advantages or disadvantages in positions described by BCL, together with some guidance about exploiting such advantages. It would be natural to treat SCL but not BCL as a theory of chess, for SCL is designed to increase our knowledge of the best means of achieving certain assumed goals, just as a scientific theory may be designed to improve our ability to make accurate predictions. SCL attempts to define those means, and in doing so it presupposes BCL, which in turn prescribes the goals and the resources with which they are to be attained. SCL operates on the general assumption that it is possible, given BCL, to plan a strategy for winning games of chess by accumulating advantages and exploiting them. Such an assumption may be formulated in the general principle that theoretical advantages lead to wins. BCL may have been devised with some such aim or hope in mind, but its vocabulary would not contain terms like 'theoretical advantage', nor would its invention require the assumption of any such general principle.

Even this limited sketch of the two languages raises some obvious initial problems. In response to the claim that SCL is, but BCL is not, a theory, it may be said that even BCL may be formulated as a theory in certain circumstances. Someone who tried to formulate the rules of BCL on the basis of his observation of actual play might be regarded as developing a theory about the game, just as someone who formulates linguistic rules on the basis of an observation of speech habits might be said to be developing a linguistic theory. The point can, however, be simply conceded without at all impugning our distinction between the two languages. A more serious point arises not from the distinction between BCL and SCL, but rather from a division within each of them between what may be called their strictly linguistic as opposed to their non-linguistic components. It may be said, for example, that BCL contains both a strictly linguistic part introducing its basic vocabulary, and also a non-linguistic or prescriptive part which determines what is legal or illegal in the game. Similarly SCL may be said to contain strictly linguistic definitions of its terms, but also a non-linguistic part containing its theoretical principles.

Such distinctions, however, seem impossible to make out. Sometimes, no doubt, a rule of BCL may be regarded as prior to another, so that the latter could not be understood without having understood the former. It would scarcely be possible, for example, to understand a rule allocating initial positions to pieces on the board without having had some prior knowledge of the board and of the named positions on it. But such particular priorities do not generally reflect a fixed order of presentation among all the rules. Nor if they did should we have to assume that at some point in the order the rules ceased to be linguistic and became instead legal or prescriptive.

Consider, for example, the following as rules of BCL:

K 1   The knight is a piece now usually distinguished by the figure of a horse's head. (The definition given in the *Oxford English Dictionary*.)

K 2   Each player has two knights. The white knights occupy squares b1 and g1 in the initial position; the black knights occupy squares b8 and g8.

K 3   A knight may move to any square diagonally adjacent to a square adjacent but not diagonally adjacent to its present square, provided that the square to which it moves is not itself adjacent to its present square.

If we were to ask which of these rules is prior to the others, or which is strictly linguistic, it would scarcely be possible to decide. Although K 1 is the criterion cited in the dictionary, it is plainly a less reliable indicator of knighthood than either K 2 or K 3. Any conflict between K 1 and the others would be easily resolved by rejecting K 1, but a conflict between K 2 and K 3 would be difficult to resolve within the game. Thus K 2 and K 3 rather than K 1 are rules of BCL, and generate within it a series of necessary truths such as 'If this is a white knight, it occupies either b1 or g1 in the initial position', or 'From the initial position the black knight on g8 can move only either to e7, f6, or h6'. But it is not possible to allocate any definite order of priority between K 2 and K 3; nor if it were would that provide a clear reason for regarding either as linguistic rather than legal. Both provide, within the language, criteria for the ascription of knighthood, and both also determine what is legal or illegal in the game.

In a similar way it might be thought that a distinction could be drawn in SCL between its strictly linguistic and its theoretical principles. We might expect to be able to draw a clear line between formal definitions of its key terms, such as 'spatial advantage', 'temporal advantage', 'better pawn structure', 'initiative', 'positional sacrifice', and the theoretical principles which are to be discovered from the game. But it is, once more, difficult to make out such a distinction. Consider, for example, the following as rules of SCL:

S 1   A player has a spatial advantage if his pieces occupy more of the board than do his opponent's pieces.

S 2   In a closed position a player with a manœuvrable knight against a bishop has a spatial advantage.

We might be initially inclined to regard S 1 as a purely formal definition of 'spatial advantage', and to treat S 2 as a more specific theoretical principle which indicates an unobvious way of satisfying the general definition. This view might be supported by claiming that S 1 is obvious and tells us nothing new, whereas S 2 might have had to be learned laboriously from chess play. Or, finally, it might be said that while S 2 is revisable in the light of experience or of other conflicting principles, S 1 is invulnerable to such revision.

But once such an initial distinction has been proposed, it is hard to see how it can be sustained. S 1 may seem obvious as an account of spatial advantage because it trades so heavily on our everyday ideas of spatial occupancy, whereas S 2 does not. But there is after all no good reason to believe that everyday ideas of spatial occupancy can be simply carried over from everyday life into chess. We may be misled into accepting S 1 just because we have overlooked the need to interpret it in specifically chess terms. The key idea of occupying space in S 1 is consequently ambiguous and may need to be refined in the light of other more specific principles such as S 2. The ambiguity perhaps means that S 1 may come to be retained in the face of difficulties simply by continually adjusting the sense of 'spatial occupation'. But this kind of shield against experience reveals

S 1's inadequacy rather than its strength, and does not in any case serve to distinguish it from S 2. If S 1 is left vague it will be misleading; and if it simply comes to reflect other more specific principles it will be redundant. In either case it may need to be eliminated in favour of such principles as S 2. Both S 1 and S 2 may be said to offer criteria for identifying spatial advantages of one sort or another. It seems a somewhat arbitrary procedure to nominate certain of these criteria as specifically linguistic and others not.

Whatever the internal structure of BCL and SCL may be, their relationship to each other is fairly clear. As far as the recording of games is concerned BCL is primarily descriptive. Its resources produce such claims as (1) 'Black has four pawns on h7, g6, f5, and a7, a king on g7, and a rook on f7'. SCL on the other hand enables us to make claims such as (2) 'Black stands better: he has a slight material advantage and the initiative. His pawn structure is superior and he has the two bishops'. Type (2) claims are plainly related to those of type (1); they will indeed naturally be based upon them. But claims of type (2) are not purely descriptive. Certainly they describe features of Black's position in terms of the vocabulary of SCL, but they also evaluate the position against that of his opponent. There is also in such claims a reference to prediction, of an indirect kind. We could not strictly infer that Black will win if he has a theoretical advantage, but we may infer that he ought to win or will win with correct play. Such a prediction could be used as a test of the type (2) evaluation only by reference to the notion of correct play which is itself defined in terms of SCL.

Such a relationship between the two sets of claims, or languages, satisfies the conditions for what has been called 'standard scepticism'. Among the expressions of BCL are true descriptions of positions in chess which form the basis for an assessment of theoretical advantage. Such an evaluation is normally made by means of the constitutive principles of SCL. If we ask whether there is a simple deductive relation between the two kinds of claim the answer appears to be just as negative as it was in the earlier cases. If this were not so, then there would strictly be no need for a separate language apart from BCL. But at present, for example in devising a computer programme for chess playing, a language such as SCL has to be used. If we consider whether the relation is inductive the same difficulties arise as in the earlier cases. In order to provide an empirical correlation between basic positions and theoretical advantages we have to gain independent access to the latter. But the idea of identifying such an advantage without recourse to a basic position seems at least as confused as that of identifying an external object without recourse to sense perception.

The position is much the same with respect to the general principle underlying SCL, namely that theoretical advantages lead to wins. Such a principle seems to have a similar role in the development of chess strategy to that of the principle that the future resembles the past in the development of inductive policies. It stands as a general expression of belief in the possibility of SCL, so that to justify it would be to justify SCL itself. But the principle is not a logical truth. It would clearly be false of a game like snakes and ladders; and if it were false of chess, then there would be no rational strategy for accumulating and exploiting theoretical advantages. But just because of the special relationship between the principle and SCL itself, the former cannot be justified in any simple empirical way by correlating theoretical advantages and wins. Such an attempt could be carried out only by identifying theoretical advantages, but it is precisely this which is at issue. The circularity of such an attempt reminds us that the principle does not simply express an empirical correlation between independent items. Rather it is a pre-condition of SCL itself, and consequently a pre-condition of establishing or rejecting such simple inductive correlations. The principle stands as a token figurehead for the specific principles of SCL which in turn provide criteria for the recognition of theoretical advantages in particular positions. It also, no doubt, encourages chess players and theorists to find and modify such principles and criteria.

The same conclusions that were drawn from the earlier cases may also be drawn here. In one way it is certainly futile to question the whole institution of SCL. Certainly a chess player whose sceptical doubts infect his actual play gives himself no chance of securing advantages, if they really exist. But, as in the earlier cases, the point of the argument is theoretical and general rather than practical and particular. The sceptic's doubts are not like those which consume the chess player's time in the interpretation of a difficult position. For the sceptic makes no distinction between these practical doubts and certainties. But to adopt a theoretical viewpoint does not prevent the doubt from being empty. If a sceptic were to legislate, for example, that 'know' may be used of an advantage only where a forced win can be demonstrated, this by itself would be an empty gesture. Or again, to insist impossibly on the identification of theoretical advantages without reference to basic positions is to utter irresoluble and empty doubts. There are not, separately, positions and advantages, but only advantageous and disadvantageous positions.

Nevertheless, as in the earlier cases, the sceptic's argument points usefully to certain features of such languages and their institution. The argument shows, for example, that there is a difference between testing empirical correlations within a language and justifying the language itself. It points in this case to the apparent need for constitutive principles to interpret observed positions, without which the development of chess strategy would be impossible. Empirical correlations of the kind required in the argument presuppose the apparatus of SCL and cannot, therefore, be treated as an independent inductive justification for it. This is not to say that particular principles of SCL cannot themselves be revised or tested. Only to test any particular principle will be to assume others, and will involve a complex interaction between SCL and actual results in play.

The argument points in this way to the descriptive task of articulating such a language as SCL, and of explaining how it may change in response to criticism. If that were all the force left to the sceptic, then there would be little reason to talk of doubt at all. But, just as in the earlier cases, the same mixture of genuine and spurious doubt arises here. We might say that a decisive justification for SCL would be a justification for all its principles together. But we do not have, after all, a final or definitive version of SCL, nor even any clear idea of what such a version would be like. It is not known whether currently accepted principles might not all be redundant, either because it is not possible to identify correct play beyond a certain point or because there is some simple technique for guaranteeing a win from some opening move. There is, consequently, still room for doubt and criticism in establishing the form and limits of SCL itself. Such a task provides a legitimate residual doubt arising from the sceptic's argument, but it can be carried out only by refining and rejecting principles within the system itself. There may seem, in the case of a finite game like chess, to be at least the possibility of a decisive outcome in such a task, for example in the successful formulation of a computer programme. If such outcomes seem impossible in the earlier open-ended examples such as that of induction itself, then this only underlines the dangers of emptiness in the sceptic's case.

7

ORDINARY LANGUAGE

So-called linguistic philosophy is now commonly identified with a doctrine about the primacy of ordinary language. In one way it is natural that this should be so, for the interest in ordinary language is historically the latest development in the philosophical revolution. But it should be remembered that an interest in language was just as prominent among logical positivists, or Cambridge philosophers such as Russell, who would nevertheless have ascribed a primacy not to ordinary language but to the technical languages of logic or the sciences. The whole revolutionary movement from Frege to Austin demonstrates a central interest in language. Only in its most recent form has that interest been narrowed down to ordinary language.

No doubt it would be historically valuable to trace all the motives and arguments which prompted this shift in philosophical interest. Certainly they, like the interest in ordinary language itself, would be too complex to record comprehensively here. If the transition appears simple it is perhaps because it can be so closely associated with one particular philosopher in the revolution. In Wittgenstein's *Philosophical Investigations* (Oxford, 1953) it is easy to find passages which question or even reject his own earlier emphasis on the formal apparatus of Russell's and Frege's logic. In paragraph 23, for example, he says

It is interesting to compare the multiplicity of the tools in language, and of the ways they are used, the multiplicity of kinds of word and sentence, with what logicians have said about the structure of language. (Including the author of the *Tractatus Logico-Philosophicus*.)

The implied comparison between the complexity of language and the artificial simplicity of logic was echoed by many later linguistic philosophers. But this natural symbol of the move away from technical and towards non-technical language is also in some respects misleading. Even in his earlier work Wittgenstein had not apparently held the naive view that ordinary language was simply inferior to, and required to be corrected by, logic. In the *Tractatus* he had, for example, expressed the view that 'All propositions of our colloquial language are actually, just as they are, logically completely in order' (5.5563), a view which he further elaborates in the *Investigations* (para. 98 ff). And in the later work he constantly formulates the slogans of his therapeutic philosophy in terms of the dangers inherent in language; saying, for example, 'Philosophy is a battle against the bewitchment of our intelligence by means of language' (para. 109). Wittgenstein's own somewhat epigrammatic presentation of the transition is complex and not easy to understand, and his influence in any case was not the only stimulus leading philosophers in the direction of ordinary language.

Before considering some of these motives something should be said of the idea of ordinary language itself. There is a strong temptation to associate ordinary language with natural language, but these could certainly not be simply identified. For one thing a natural language, such as English, itself contains a set of technical vocabularies. It would be a mistake to make a simple opposition between English and the language of physics, as though these were two distinct languages of the same general kind. Claims in physics may generally be expressed in English as in other natural languages of a certain degree of complexity. But part of the point of identifying ordinary language was precisely to contrast such specialist technical terminology with that commonly used in colloquial speech. Ordinary language could not be identified with English, or any other natural language, but at best only with its non-technical, colloquial part. But even such a partial identification would be wrong, for ordinary language was thought of as notation-free, that is, as unrestricted to any particular natural language. In order to identify claims in such a notation-free language some representative notation has nevertheless to be used. But if English was chosen generally as such a representative the language it represented was designed to cover any equivalent translation of those claims in any other natural language.

Some of the dangers and misconceptions arising from this notation-free device have been already noted (in Chapter 4). An additional hazard, which was commonly put as an objection to ordinary language philosophy, arises from the special features of the representative language. Discriminations which appear quite untechnical in one language may nevertheless appear technical in another. It is, consequently, not easy to mark out exactly the scope of ordinary language. But, more than this, the representative language may have its own peculiarities which may not be matched in other possible representatives. There is no general reason to suppose that every claim in any other natural language can be adequately translated into English. Any conclusions drawn from one representative may have only a limited and not a universal scope.

Some of the motives for the shift of interest to non-technical language were also mentioned earlier (in Chapter 2). One way of looking at it would be to stress two reasons for rejecting the logical positivists' optimism about their own philosophical programme. Positivists like Reichenbach evidently held the paradoxical beliefs that philosophy was both distinct from science and yet had also become scientific. The paradox may be partially resolved in the doctrine of rational reconstruction. For in one way the task of reformulating theories in the technical language of logic might be regarded both as scientific and as distinct from science. It was distinct from science in that it was a second-order activity relating to a first-order scientific theory; but the logical apparatus used for the task might itself be held to have become scientific. Certainly this latter claim represented and expressed a common optimism about the status and development of logic.

Subsequently that optimism was somewhat eroded. Wittgenstein's doubts about the models for language derived from logic seemed to be confirmed by other investigations of language. Perhaps the most striking of these further investigations was Strawson's criticism of Russell's theory of descriptions, which itself had seemed to an earlier generation a model of philosophical analysis.[1] Strawson's examination of the ways in which definite descriptions are used in ordinary speech seemed to cast doubt on the ability of Russell's logic to handle adequately such features of ordinary language. It echoed the claims made by Wittgenstein about the complexity and variety of even such elementary linguistic forms. It would be quite wrong to think that ordinary language philosophers simply abandoned or rejected logic. On the contrary they continued to employ its techniques, and often modelled their own classifications on it. But

[1] Russell's original paper 'On Denoting' appeared in *Mind*, 1905. Strawson's reply 'On Referring' appeared in *Mind*, 1950. See also Strawson's *Introduction to Logical Theory* (London, 1952), especially ch. 3, § II.

they no longer expected the technical apparatus of logic to give a complete picture of ordinary linguistic uses. They devised new classifications and uncovered new phenomena, such as Austin's performative utterances and the whole range of speech acts, to mark these more pragmatic aspects of language.[1]

This line of development indicates one kind of primacy that came to be attached to ordinary language. The limitations found in logic stimulated an independent enquiry into the variety of uses found in ordinary language. Ordinary language came to be given a priority simply as a topic for investigation, as a datum for study in its own right. In some ways this change of direction fitted in well with the earlier views that philosophy was quite distinct from science and yet should also be scientific. Ordinary language is more accessible than the languages of science, while the new subject-matter was still both linguistic and second-order. But the change also involved a radical reinterpretation of the positivist doctrine. For philosophy was now distinct from science not in virtue of its second-order reconstruction of science, but in the much stronger sense that it had nothing to do with science. Even the requirement that philosophy should be systematic or scientific reappeared transformed in connection with the new subject-matter. Warnock's reference to the acquisition in philosophy of systematic conceptual knowledge is a natural expression of this requirement. But it testifies to a belief in the inadequacy of formal logic to provide such a system, which the positivists generally would not have held.

This interest in ordinary language as a new topic for investigation involved a distinct change from the traditional topics of philosophy. But the second general reason for rejecting the positivists' optimistic programme actually stimulated a return to certain traditional topics. The positivists had employed their verification test as a means of eliminating many traditional problems in philosophy as meaningless. According to this criterion any meaningful claim must be either necessarily true (or false), or else empirically verifiable (or falsifiable). But the criterion rejects as meaningless not only philosophical claims but also whole areas of quite ordinary discourse as well. A moral claim of the form 'You ought to confess', for example, is not necessarily true (or false), and seems not to be verifiable (or falsifiable) by reference to empirical facts. Yet such ordinary moral claims do not seem to be meaningless either. The blanket rejection of large areas of discourse as meaningless according to the verification test

[1] See J. L. Austin, *Philosophical Papers*, ch. 10, and *How to Do Things With Words* (Oxford, 1962). See also J. R. Searle, *Speech Acts*.

ultimately reflected rather on the validity of the test itself than on the meaningfulness of the rejected claims.

This second disillusion naturally stimulated interest in the operation of such rejected languages as those of morality, aesthetics, or religion. In so far as these languages could be thought of as non-technical it also reinforced the interest in the new topic of ordinary language. But it also stimulated a renewed interest in traditional problems which the verification test had dismissed as meaningless. In most cases the interest lay less in merely reviving the problems than in attempting to find some better way of eliminating or resolving them. The positivist rejection of problems as meaningless gave way to the technique of therapeutic treatment. One example of such a technique can be seen in the attempts to refute scepticism by an appeal to ordinary language. And this points to a second kind of primacy that was attached to ordinary language, namely a primacy as an arbiter in philosophical disputes. In general the assumption in all the appeals to ordinary language, and the paradigm case arguments, was that whenever a philosopher makes a claim which runs counter to common sense our ordinary language must be appealed to as an arbiter. Since it was generally also assumed that our ordinary language actually guaranteed our common-sense beliefs the arbiter might appear less as an impartial judge than as a fixed jury. Nevertheless it was in somewhat this way that ordinary language came to be used as an antisceptical weapon. It is these two kinds of primacy attached to ordinary language, as an arbiter in philosophical disputes and as a subject-matter in its own right, that will be discussed in the remainder of this chapter.

1. *Ordinary language as a philosophical arbiter*

Something has been said already of the appeal to ordinary language in certain sceptical arguments. But the appeal was treated there quite summarily and certainly did scant justice to the arguments in favour of it. Even now those arguments cannot be treated comprehensively for the technique had a long and complex history in the revolution. There is, however, one valuable representative version of the argument which contains a reference to almost all the salient points in it. Malcom's paper 'Moore and Ordinary Language'[1] is one of the earliest but also one of the best statements of the argument. It has also the historical merit of linking the appeal to ordinary language with Moore and also with later linguistic philosophers.

[1] In P. Schilpp (Ed.), *The Philosophy of G. E. Moore* (Evanston and Chicago, 1942). The paper is reprinted in R. Rorty (Ed.), *The Linguistic Turn*.

Malcolm begins by identifying the kind of philosophical problem he is concerned with, namely those in which philosophers appear to deny common-sense beliefs. They may claim that things which we ordinarily believe to exist, such as external objects, do not exist; or that what we ordinarily take to be real, such as space and time, is not real; or that beliefs which we ordinarily think justified, such as inductive beliefs, are not justified. Malcolm takes the general view that such denials of common sense could be supported in only two ways. Either it must be shown that our common-sense beliefs are empirically false, or else it must be shown that they are self-contradictory. But he claims that neither demonstration can be effective, for philosophers do not offer any empirical evidence of falsity, and no expression with an ordinary use could be self-contradictory. This bare dilemma, however, shows only the outline of Malcolm's position. Most of the weight of the argument is borne by his general claim that 'Ordinary language is correct language', which in turn is supported by two subsidiary arguments. In the first of these Malcolm argues that the way in which the disputed terms must be learned, by reference to paradigm cases, guarantees the truth of their application. In the second he argues that if we construe the sceptic as making a recommendation to change our use of the disputed terms, then his recommendations are empty and would achieve nothing.

In introducing the first argument Malcolm considers an objection to his view that ordinary language is correct language. It may be said that it does not follow from the fact that an expression is used in ordinary language that it is ever truly applied to some thing. He goes on

The expression 'There's a ghost' has a descriptive use. It is, in my use of the phrase, an ordinary expression; and it does not follow from the fact that it is an ordinary expression that there ever have been any ghosts. But it is important to note that people can learn the meaning of the word 'ghost' without actually seeing any ghosts. That is, the meaning of the word 'ghost' can be explained to them in terms of the meanings of words which they already know. It seems to me that there is an enormous difference in this respect between the learning of the word 'ghost' and the learning of expressions like 'earlier', 'later', 'to the left of', 'behind', 'above', 'material things', 'it is possible that', 'it is certain that'. The difference is that, whereas you can teach a person the meaning of the word 'ghost' without showing him an instance of the true application of the word, you cannot teach a person the meaning of these other expressions without showing him instances of the true application of those expressions.[1]

[1] *The Linguistic Turn*, pp. 119–20.

It was suggested earlier that such an argument might work for simple observational terms, perhaps colour words, but not for complex terms. Malcolm's argument rests on a distinction between simple terms which can be completely learned only from exposure to ostensive instances, and complex terms whose meaning may be given and taught through verbal definitions. The argument seems plausible for simple observational words because in their case any theoretical meaning seems to be reduced to a minimum. It is as though the meaning of a term like 'red' can be taken up simply through exposure to particular instances of its application. But in the case of complex terms it is always possible to explain their meaning verbally; and in the case of complex theoretical terms it may even be necessary to explain part of their meaning in this way.

These contrasts may be illustrated from any complex vocabulary. It may be necessary in chess to teach the colours of pieces by reference to ostensive procedures, but a complex term like 'knight' may be taught by giving a verbal account, and the theoretical term like 'positional advantage' may require such a verbal account. Even if it were possible to teach the meaning of 'knight' simply by reference to instances of its application, it is hard to believe that it would be possible to teach the meaning of 'positional advantage' merely by exposing someone to instances of its application. Again some terms, such as diagnostic words, may contain a necessary reference to theoretical ideas in their meaning. Let us suppose that the disease we now know as leprosy was once diagnosed as 'King's Evil'. Such a diagnostic term may contain as part of its meaning a reference to the aetiology and possible cure of the condition, in this case a reference to the way the disorder might be brought on or cured by monarchs. Certainly part of the term's meaning must lie in its discrimination between what we would call lepers and non-lepers, but a man who knew only this about it could not be said fully to understand the meaning of the term. A reference to paradigm cases of its application may even be necessary in teaching the diagnosis, but a theoretical background is also necessary. We could not argue here that because of the essential reference to paradigm cases the term's application cannot be questioned and must be correct. For the term may embody in its meaning a wholly mistaken account of disease in general and of this condition in particular. The fact that the term may be used consistently to discriminate lepers from non-lepers does not mean that its use is correct, or that we are prevented from passing on its misconceptions to future generations.

Malcolm's argument then requires that the disputed terms he

cites are neither complex nor theoretical, but simple observational terms. Judged by this standard it is simply not convincing to regard terms such as 'space', 'time', 'material object', 'certainty' and 'possibility' as simple observational terms. On the contrary in every case they seem to contain a reference to a complex theoretical background which may accommodate changes running counter to our common-sense beliefs. If this should not seem so, for example in the case of space and time, it may be because in this case alone Malcolm replaces the original disputed terms with more specific spatial or temporal relations. Or again, in the case of space and time it may seem inevitable to advert to particular cases just because it seems impossible to conceive of an experience which is not spatio-temporal. But if terms like 'chair' and 'table' are complex by comparison with a word like 'red', then such terms as 'material thing' or 'certainty' appear to be even more complex and theoretical. Malcolm may be right to argue that all these terms require a reference to paradigm cases, or that we should not be said to understand their meaning fully if we could not discriminate between paradigms of their application and non-application. But this does not establish that there are any things to which the words truly apply. This would be established only if the paradigms involved also simple ostensive instances. If they involve theoretical considerations at all, then they may in the light of theory revision be regarded as mistakenly applied to those paradigms.

It may be said that in any genuine case of theory revision there must be a reference to empirical evidence, and that Malcolm explicitly allows for this, only claiming that at least philosophers never offer such support. But there are two strong replies to this. First, if Malcolm's argument were correct and the application of the disputed terms were beyond question or revision, then he would be committed to saying that nothing could count against them, not even any empirical evidence. Second, however, even though it may be right to insist that empirical evidence is ultimately needed to support changes in theory, such revisions are not quite simply or directly related to such evidence. A theory should be a complex structure which may be shielded from counter-evidence over a long period. By the same token revisions may be proposed without direct empirical support as an intellectual exercise in order to see what such a theory would be like, or how it might be articulated. It is true that philosophical sceptics have rarely been involved in the implications of their proposed revisions as they should have been. But such a complaint is quite different from Malcolm's objection that such changes could never be justified, whether proposed by philosophers or not.

So far Malcolm's objections to the sceptic rest on his argued conviction that since ordinary language is correct the sceptic's proposed changes in it must be incorrect. In his second argument he moves to the next stage and tries to show that even if we were to accept a sceptic's recommendation it would be pointless or empty and could achieve nothing. In the previous chapter it was admitted that such a claim can be made out for some cases, but Malcolm's argument is designed to show that it is true of all. Malcolm considers a case in which a philosopher in saying that all words are vague is recommending a new use for the contrast between clarity and vagueness according to which no word can be regarded as clear. He says

It is important to see that by such a move we should have gained nothing whatever. The word in our revised language would have to do double duty. The word 'vague' would have to perform the function previously performed by two words 'vague' and 'clear'. But it could not perform this function. For it was essential to the meaning of the word 'vague', in its previous use, that vagueness was *contrasted* with clearness. In the revised language vagueness could be contrasted with nothing. The word 'vague' would simply be dropped as a useless word. And we should be compelled to adopt into the revised language a new pair of words with which to express the same distinctions formerly expressed by the words 'clear' and 'vague'. The revision of our language would have accomplished nothing.[1]

It is necessary to distinguish two different theses in this argument. One is that the proposed revision would make no difference at all to the situation. Such a view expresses a general thesis about the emptiness or neutrality of linguistic change. The other thesis is that even though it might make a difference the change has no value or importance. Both views have been considered in connection with Ayer's proposed revisions of language. There it was argued that proposed revisions might be of no value, but that there was no general justification for the view that they were all quite empty. Revising our diagnostic language to replace 'King's Evil' with 'leprosy' might make a considerable difference both to the theory of medicine and to the treatment of patients. Nevertheless Malcolm's view seems to be that there is some quite general objection to all such proposals.

Malcolm's basic point is that in the revised language the word 'vague' would have to perform the function previously performed by the word 'clear' as well as its own new function. But such double

[1] *The Linguistic Turn*, p. 122.

duty is, according to Malcolm, impossible, since it was essential to the function of 'vague' that it should be contrasted with 'clear'. But here Malcolm is surely wrong to suppose that the word 'vague' is taking over the *function* of the word 'clear'. All that is happening is that the word 'vague' now applies to terms which were formerly thought to be clear. Its function, we may say, has always been to classify words, among other things, according to some standard in which there is a contrast between clarity and vagueness. This function it still retains in the new language, at least so long as there is some idea of a standard of clarity that words might meet, whether any actually do or not. The fact that no words at present meet this new standard does not prevent us from having, and attaching a sense to, the contrast between vagueness and clarity. The fact that we now regard all British rivers as polluted because we have raised our standards of non-pollution would not prevent us from attaching sense to the contrast between being polluted and being unpolluted.

Malcolm, however, claims that in the new language the word 'vague' can no longer be contrasted with the word 'clear', but it is plain that this point rests on an equivocation. In one way we cannot in the new language contrast any clear words with vague words, since there are no clear words with which to contrast the latter. But, in another way, the contrast is still there as it is in the example of the polluted rivers so long as we have some idea of what a clear word would be. Generally we may say that the word 'vague' still has a function and a meaning so long as there is the possibility of a contrasted case. It is not necessary that there should actually be instances of both terms in the contrast. It is not necessary that there should actually be any supersonic air liners in order to give a sense to the term 'subsonic air liner'. Malcolm's claim that we should have to drop the revised use and revert to the original is simply unsupported, though no doubt if this reversion did take place we might agree that the original recommendation was empty or ineffective. The argument certainly does not establish generally that every such recommendation will be empty or ineffective.

These arguments appear to be inadequate, but it is worth asking how it is that Malcolm came to overlook the possibility and importance of linguistic change. Two answers are suggested by his paper. First Malcolm employs the rigid division between factual and linguistic considerations, which I have argued to be misleading or wrong. More than that, however, it is evident that what Malcolm means by factual considerations are those relevant to a particular case according to current standards or principles. The suggestion is

that a sceptic could show the disputed claims to be factually false only by showing that we believed mistakenly that they satisfied our existing standards. In arguing for the claim that all words are vague, for example, it would have to be shown that we had simply mistaken the relevant features of words formerly thought clear. Any change in our standards or revision of our criteria would then be regarded as non-empirical. But such a conclusion is misleading in two ways. It suggests, quite wrongly, that the only way of justifying such revisions would be to show that existing standards are self-contradictory. And it suggests, equally wrongly, that changes of standards or criteria have no reference to facts and so must be empty.

Second, however, despite the fact that Malcolm's arguments strictly rule out any such revisions, he might wish to draw a sharp distinction between philosophical and other such proposals. There is no doubt that the former may sometimes be empty, and some temptation to think that they must all be empty. Moore's own technique, which Malcolm is officially explaining, undoubtedly had a value in its context as a revolutionary counter to the pretentious speculative idealism of the period. But the division between philosophy and other disciplines is not, if the argument here is correct, either clear or exclusive. Philosophical recommendations may have implications for other disciplines. There is no general reason to suppose that they, or the arguments for them, occur in an intellectual vacuum. When we talk of philosophical arguments, or claims, or proposals we are not talking of a range of ideas to be judged by their own unique standards. We are talking only of arguments, claims, or proposals which happen to be issued by philosophers, and are to be judged by the same standards as any others. It is by reference to such general standards that some philosophical recommendations should be judged empty, but there is no reason why they should all suffer this fate. Already by the time Malcolm wrote his paper the targets of Moore's own attack were discredited. But even if there is some historical justification for Moore it can scarcely be applied to his successors.

2. *Ordinary languega as a philosophical topic*

Despite the fact that arguments like Malcolm's, with his background assumptions, are inadequate the appeal to ordinary language and the paradigm case argument have some value. They do not provide a final refutation of the philosophical positions they were directed against, but they begin to make clear the complex nature of the sceptic's doubts and the ways in which they may escape the pitfalls of emptiness. Even beyond that the arguments point to two further developments in linguistic philosophy. In the first place they offer ordinary language as a datum for further investigation. Even in the sceptical arguments one substantial issue lay in explaining or formulating the meanings of the disputed terms. If there is to be any useful debate about the unwarranted or fictitious elements a disputed term contains in its meaning, then it is plainly necessary to find out what its meaning is. One way of pursuing such an enquiry would be simply to examine the ways in which the term is used. In pointing to the paradigm applications of disputed terms the appeal to ordinary language offered a material for resolving such issues. Ordinary language in this context has ceased to be a judge in philosophical disputes and has become instead a key witness. It has ceased, in Austin's phrase, to be the last word, though it still remains the first.[1]

Second, however, the appeal to ordinary language offered a slightly different subject-matter for investigation. For the idea of an ordinary language was inevitably associated with the system of common-sense beliefs. Strictly speaking the appeal to ordinary language was an appeal to common sense, as Moore correctly saw and described it. Ordinary language contains, just as English does, pairs of expressions such as 'External objects exist' and 'Time is real' as well as such other pairs as 'External objects do not exist' and 'Time is unreal'. As far as ordinary language goes no preference is expressed for one of these pairs rather than another. Common sense on the other hand feels a decided preference for the first rather than the second pair. Hence it is natural to regard common sense as a theory, or at least as a set of beliefs related to ordinary language in somewhat the way in which a chemical theory is related to its basic vocabulary and syntax. But in that case common-sense beliefs might themselves be investigated just as a scientific theory may. Just as in the case of a theory there may be a question about the structure of such beliefs, or of the principles which govern them, or some detailed issue about the meaning of a particular term.

There is, however, still something odd about regarding common sense as a theory. It might almost be regarded instead as that which is opposed to theory. We might allow that any theory actually requires a language, but still deny that the converse holds. It may be possible for a language to be related to no theory at all, and it may be said that ordinary language is just such a language. Certainly common sense can scarcely be treated as a technical, unified, or

[1] *Philosophical Papers*, p. 133.

articulated theory. At best it covers a vast range of disconnected topics in a loosely organised way. On the other hand we think of common sense, as we think of theories, as containing beliefs or commitment to belief. Equally though we may wish to draw a distinction between language and theory it is plain that there are intimate connections between them. A language may, or may not, enable us to formulate certain theories. In Ayer's illusionless language we should not recognise the existence of illusions, and could not therefore even begin to consider how they might be explained. The dividing line between the principles in some system of beliefs which we may wish to regard as linguistic and others will certainly be blurred. Linguistic philosophers, for example, were right to point to the dual role of paradigm applications of some term in a language. On one side such paradigm applications may guide or instruct our linguistic capacities, but on the other they are expressed in the form of contingent claims. Such paradigm claims could not be regarded as formulating properly the meaning of the particular words, but at least they indicate again the close link between language and theory, or language and contingent belief. In this way common sense may come to be conceived as a basic and primitive theory, or set of theories.

Such a system of beliefs expressed in ordinary language is generally more accessible than the technical theories of science, but there was another motive for its investigation. It may be said that common sense or ordinary language is in some way prior to, or more basic than, those technical constructions. A motive of this sort was expressed in Austin's claim that

our common stock of words embodies all the distinctions men have found worth drawing, and the connexions they have found worth making, in the lifetimes of many generations; these surely are likely to be more numerous, more sound, . . . and more subtle . . . than any you or I are likely to think up in our arm-chairs of an afternoon.[1]

Ordinary language may be regarded as historically prior to the technical languages which deviate from it. It may even be regarded as logically prior in providing for those languages a background against which to understand those deviations and in terms of which ultimately to justify them. For ordinary language may also be regarded

---

[1] *Philosophical Papers*, p. 130. Those who regard Austin as a paradigm of ordinary language philosophy will, however, have to disregard the fact that he also includes in his material for study the technical systems of the law, and the technical theories of psychology. op. cit., pp. 135–7.

E

as containing a basic observation language by reference to which even technical theories may have to be supported and understood.

There is no doubt that some of these claims for priority can be made out. It is scarcely possible to deny that ordinary language provides a basic non-technical vocabulary from which deviant technical terminologies may be developed. Equally our common-sense beliefs may be superseded by theoretical developments. There seems little merit in clinging to a system of beliefs as an object of study for that reason, if it has already been superseded. Even if it has some formal interest like a historical study of discarded scientific theories, such an interest must be limited by the unsystematic and unrigorous character of common sense itself. It may be held that an enquiry into principles which are presupposed in all our experience might justify an interest in common sense.[1] But if such background principles genuinely govern the whole of our experience, then they will not be exclusive to common sense. They may be located through an investigation of common sense, but they might equally have been found in an investigation of technical theories. Such principles, even if required for common sense, can hardly be said themselves to belong to common sense; nor, if the claims made for them are true, can they be in any way unique to it.

It was, however, noted earlier that such an interest in common sense as a theory was not essentially involved in the alternative development. Under the influence of the paradigm case argument what was to be investigated was the meaning of specific words in a language, not so much for any priority they may have over corresponding technical terms but simply for the sake of clarification. Such an interest was certainly influenced in its choice of words to clarify by their relation to philosophical issues. In the case of Austin's work on excuses (*Philosophical Papers*, ch. 6), for example the words were chosen for their ultimate relevance to philosophical views about action, freedom and responsibility. But Austin's plausible view was that we could scarcely expect to make much headway in these matters until we were much clearer about the detailed meaning of the relevant words. It has always been admitted that the task of preliminary clarification is typically philosophical. Such a view was, for example, even indicated in the pre-revolutionary Cartesian picture of the subject. The linguistic version of the claim in the revolution may have been in some respects misleading, but it

[1] Perhaps Strawson's descriptive metaphysics in his *Individuals* (London, 1959), should be interpreted in this way.

also demonstrated a more technical and more precise interest in clarification than any earlier philosophers had shown.

It has, however, been pointed out that we should not necessarily think of such clarification as exclusively linguistic. Austin himself acknowledged the point when he said

When we examine what we say when, what words we should use in what situations, we are looking again not *merely* at words (or 'meanings' whatever they may be) but also at the realities we use the words to talk about (*Philosophical Papers*, p. 130).

It is consequently not surprising that Austin should also have promoted a picture of philosophy as essentially involved with other disciplines. Not only did he accept as part of his material the technical data of law or psychology, but he also regarded philosophers as helping, with other theorists, to develop new areas of enquiry. In his case the suggestion was that philosophers and other theorists might help in the birth of a new science of language (*Philosophical Papers*, pp. 179–80). The sharp division between philosophy and science was mitigated in his case by a recognition of a period when philosophy and other disciplines might overlap. But it is difficult to see the justification for a distinction between the birth of a new science and its subsequent progress. Perhaps he had the view that after its establishment a science develops only in terms of factual investigations. Taken in one way such a view claims that after its birth the development of a science is, in Kuhn's sense, eternally normal and never revolutionary. There is, however, no good reason to take such a view. Sciences do not complete their development at birth. Their subsequent progress may involve disputes about, and revisions of, their background principles which are just as revolutionary and just as philosophical as the problems which led to their birth. If there is an area of philosophical enquiry within these other disciplines, then it remains there even after the science has been established.

Such an enquiry into the meanings of particular words presupposes some general account of meaning. If no such account is available then a mere record of word uses will tell us nothing definite about meaning. For without such an account there is no ground for separating those uses of a word which are relevant to its meaning from those which are not. The constitutive principles of such an account enable us to interpret the empirical data of word use in terms of meaning. Otherwise we have a typically sceptical situation with two sets of claims, about word use and about meaning, and no adequate means of moving from one to the other. Of course we have at our disposal the ordinary common-sense ways in which we clarify and ascribe meaning, but the suggestion is that we should devise more satisfactory technical means of doing this. It was just such a difficulty, stressed by Quine (see pp. 65–78), which seemed to cast doubt on the distinction drawn earlier between necessary and contingent truth. But the problem of revising our criteria for meaning does not cast any doubt on the distinction in general. So long as there is some way of ascribing an unambiguous meaning to a word, even if it is not the way we now employ, the subsidiary distinction will remain. We may, in the light of a revision of our criteria, revise our initial classification of particular claims, but still retain the general contrast. It is not necessary, in order to defend the original distinction, to deny any possibility of revising our criteria for meaning.

It can scarcely be doubted both that our criteria for the ascription of meaning could be improved, and that linguistic philosophers in the revolution have made a contribution to our understanding of these criteria. The positivists' verification test for significance, Wittgenstein's association of meaning and use, Quine's problems about synonymy, and Austin's work on performative utterances, have all been directed at an improvement in our understanding of meaning and our criteria for ascribing it. For our purposes what is important in this line of development is to assess its relation to a general science of language, and in particular to the study of meaning. If the doctrine of philosophy's separation from science, of second-order enquiry and of a division between linguistic and factual considerations, were applied to this case we should have to say that these philosophical enquiries had no relevance to the empirical study of meaning. Yet it is totally unplausible to make such a claim. Apologists might argue that the doctrine breaks down only in this one case just because philosophy is essentially a linguistic study. But philosophers are interested in this area not only because of the subject-matter, but because in it there are background problems about the criteria to be used, or about the basic principles required to constitute a theory of meaning. Such an enquiry might be undertaken by philosophers in any theoretical context which raises questions about its constitutive principles. It is not necessary for any such contribution to be made to the formulation or revision of such principles that it should be correct. On the other hand it is necessary that it should have a bearing on the empirical data of language, if it is to be genuine and valuable. Otherwise the questioning of current principles and the proposal of alternatives will not avoid the emptiness of a spurious scepticism.

It is for these reasons that Warnock's suggestion (see p. 21) of a permanent and exclusive subject-matter for philosophy in the acquisition of systematic conceptual knowledge cannot be taken at its face value. There is no general reason why philosophers should not investigate the meanings of words in a systematic way, but such an enquiry cannot be fruitful if it is exclusively confined to philosophy. If it is to be of value, then it must make some reference to the constitutive principles which govern the study of semantics, and through them to the empirical data of word use. But in that case, as Austin saw, it is an enquiry which cannot be allocated exclusively to philosophers, or to linguists either. We have noted already some of the doctrines which might nevertheless mislead philosophers into such an exclusive interest, divorced from any reference to facts. Since philosophers are concerned with language, for example, it may be held that this must be a permanent and exclusive subject-matter for them. But it has been argued that the reasons for this philosophical interest arise less from the topic itself than from the nature of the problems arising in its background principles. But problems of this kind are not confined to the area of language or meaning; they may arise in connection with any subject-matter.

Again, because philosophers are concerned with concepts rather than words, it may appear that their interest has no connection with facts of word use. But it has been argued that this attempt to separate a philosophical interest in meaning from any empirical data is seriously wrong. The device of talking about language in a notation-free way does not provide access to a totally new, exclusively philosophical, non-factual realm. It is instead merely a device to allow an extension from claims based on one notation to others which are equivalent to it. If a philosopher can elucidate the meaning of the word 'real', then it is the meaning of that word in that natural language which he elucidates. There are not two kinds of meaning, philosophical and empirical; there are only two kinds of contribution that can be made to an empirical theory of meaning, namely the proposal of constitutive principles and the recording of empirical data.

8

CONCEPTUAL SCHEMES AND

CATEGORIAL FRAMEWORKS

It has been persistently argued so far that the ideas of a language, and of a contrast between language and fact, have been employed ambiguously in recent philosophy. It has been suggested also that these ambiguities have encouraged, or concealed the operation of, a quite unnecessary restriction on the scope of philosophical tasks. For the emphasis on the acceptance of ordinary linguistic conventions, and a sharp division between linguistic and factual enquiries, have in general insulated philosophy from science and from any first-order activity. It is not the aim of the argument here to direct philosophy exclusively towards such first-order activities, and so to narrow the scope of philosophical tasks. On the contrary the intention is to widen the scope of the subject by freeing it from unnecessary restrictions.

But the ambiguities which have encouraged such restrictions are neither arbitrary nor culpable. It has been already emphasised that the terms 'fact' and 'language' are extremely complex. If the term 'language', for example, refers to one phenomenon, then it is a phenomenon of a highly complex kind, more like an extensive family than a single individual. Philosophers, like other theorists, have tried to reduce the phenomenon to manageable proportions by restricting their interest to certain branches of the family. Such an analytic enterprise is indeed necessary if the topic is to yield to enquiry at all. But it is possible that restrictions may be drawn too narrowly, or that the family may usefully be classified in ways which conflict with those restrictions. In this chapter something will be finally said of some further ramifications in these elusive notions by discussing two residual problems about facts and languages. The first problem arises out of different ways in which facts may be classified. The second arises from a natural extension of the idea of a language to cover systems of belief, and a consequent issue about linguistic or cultural relativity.

1. *Facts and non-facts*

In the earlier discussion of the contrast between fact and language (Chapter 4) the elusiveness of both terms was stressed. But there some difficulties were avoided by concentrating specifically on one such distinction which philosophers had found important. In retrospect this limitation may seem unsatisfactory. For one thing the philosophers' contrast between contingent and necessary claims is a distinction drawn within language. But it may reasonably be felt that to talk of facts, and to oppose them to language, should be to point to something independent of language itself. Indeed it has also been argued that an independent reference to facts places an important restriction on the belief that language creates or constitutes fact. It was claimed that to speak of 'identifying facts' is ambiguous in just this way. For on one side I may identify a fact by using words with a definite sense and reference, and this is a linguistic condition for such identification. But on the other side I may identify a fact only by checking that a linguistically identified state of affairs really does obtain. Without a reference to this latter non-linguistic condition the construction of languages would become entirely arbitrary.

This non-linguistic condition for the identification of facts points to a connection with observation. We naturally think of the condition as satisfied by the observation of some particular state of affairs. But once this connection has been made it is difficult to avoid the issues, previously evaded, about the classification of facts. For while it may appear obvious that there are facts corresponding to singular claims ascribing a simple property to some observable individual, it may seem doubtful whether I can observe such facts as that all grass is green, or that if the light is normal this grass is blue, or that this substance is pyretic, or that an electron has a certain angular momentum. For it may appear doubtful whether we should admit the existence of general or hypothetical or dispositional or theoretical facts.

The point may be illustrated by reference to the general distinction between facts and values. We may wish to deny that there is any fact corresponding to such claims as 'You ought to confess', or 'You ought to warn him', on the ground that they contain an autonomous moral ingredient which is not observable. Yet since the claims could be classified as contingent rather than necessary, that is, do not have their truth or falsity fully determined by a semantic convention, it may be inferred that not all contingent claims correspond to facts. In this case the difficulty may be artificially resolved by insisting that moral claims cannot be regarded as true or false, or therefore as contingently or necessarily true or false. In this way the illustration reflects a distinction between types of discourse rather than one between particular claims within the area of fact-stating discourse. But similar problems arise also in this latter area. We may be reluctant to admit moral facts because we do not believe that moral features are observable; but we may be equally reluctant to admit general, or hypothetical, or theoretical facts because we do not believe that those features are observable either. Such arguments may seem to jeopardise the independence of fact from language, for the contrasts drawn in them between facts and non-facts certainly reflect linguistic distinctions. For the moment, however, they are mentioned only because they have a bearing on two apparently conflicting classifications of facts in recent philosophy.

On one side is the contrast between necessary and contingent truth (or falsity) noted in Chapter 4. In this classification the non-facts are identified with the necessary truths in a language, and the facts are identified as a residue from these necessary claims. If we can formulate the strictly semantic principles of some language, then these will determine which expressions in the language are necessary truths. The facts will then be identified by means of the expressions whose truth (or falsity) remains undetermined by those semantic principles. On the other side, however, are classifications which appear to draw the line between fact and non-fact at a different point. These classifications, associated particularly with Quine and Kuhn, reject or disregard the first classification and insist on a functional similarity between what might be called strictly semantic principles and theoretical principles. This second classification no doubt reflects a variety of views, but Kuhn's contrast between normal and revolutionary activity can stand as their general representative. Such a classification draws its distinction between the activity of applying assumed principles to observation, and that of questioning or revising those principles.

The conflict between the two classifications may not be entirely obvious, just because they seem to operate at quite different levels. The first appears to be a classification of claims and of their logical status, while the second is rather a classification of enquiries or activities. It may not even be obvious whether the second classification involves a reference to the contrast between fact and non-facts at all. Yet there is such a reference, and it is possible in the light of this to compare their different accounts of the contrast.

In both classifications there is a reference to certain background principles which are to be contrasted with their application in observation. In the first classification it is assumed that a clear distinction can be drawn between what might be called strictly linguistic and theoretical principles, and the background principles of the classification are restricted to the former. The necessary truths which derive from these principles are contrasted with claims in which the defined terms are applied in observation. Similarly in the second classification there is a reference to background principles which are contrasted with their particular application to observation. Normal science, indeed any normal activity, consists in the assumption of such principles and the interpretation of what is observed in the light of those assumptions. If I assume certain rules of chess I may arrive at the particular conclusion that this piece is a knight. Both classifications would treat such a claim as factual, to be contrasted with the assumed principles in the background. It is worth noting, for example, that in Malcolm's paper (see pp. 121–7), his central distinction is drawn between the linguistic criteria for applying a term and the factual ascription of the term to a case which satisfies that criterion. So far Malcolm might have been subscribing to either classification. It is only when it appears that his criteria are understood to be strictly linguistic and unchangeable that he commits himself to the first classification.

So far both classifications may be represented as fundamentally similar. Moreover they both draw some plausibility from the unclarity, noted earlier, in what we regard as the observation of facts. The more complex, or general, or theoretical our terms the more we are inclined to say that the claims in which they figure are not *just* facts, or *just* contingent truths. In his *Philosophical Investigations* (para. 250) Wittgenstein asks the questions: 'Why can't a dog simulate pain? Is he too honest?'. It may be suggested that it is not just a contingent matter that a dog cannot simulate pain, but in some way a matter of the language appropriate to dumb animals. If we wish to deny that a dog can simulate pain it may be not because we believe this dog to be too honest, unlike others that one could mention, but because the whole language of honesty and dishonesty, candour and simulation, seems inapplicable. Such considerations naturally encourage, as many of Wittgenstein's other examples do, a reference to a non-factual component in claims distinct from, but applicable to, observation. In such cases, however,

E*

it is not clear whether the assumptions we habitually make should be classified among the strictly linguistic principles of the first classification, or the theoretical principles of the second.

Despite this degree of similarity it is also plain that the two classifications are different and even in conflict. The most immediate difference between them lies in the contrast between strictly linguistic and theoretical principles, which the first classification but not the second draws. Consequently while the first includes its theoretical principles in the factual side of the contrast, the second assimilates the two kinds of principle and contrasts both with observation. One simple but crude way of differentiating between the two would be to note that they draw the line between fact and non-fact at different points in the linguistic hierarchy. For the first the point of division is effectively between fact and language in a strict sense; for the second the point of division is between fact and theory. Despite the naturalness of these contrasts between fact, on one side, and language or theory on the other, it may be argued that in both cases the contrast is misleading. For if it is described as an opposition between fact and non-fact it may suggest wrongly that the background principles in both classifications are in some way invulnerable to factual test. It has been already argued that the principles of a natural language are vulnerable to fact, and this is even more obviously true of theoretical principles. Yet this is one respect in which this differentiation between the two classifications is crude. For at least some adherents of the second classification, such as Quine, explicitly take the view that all background principles are vulnerable to fact.

From the point of view of either classification the other will appear simply wrong. From the standpoint of the first, for example, the inclusion of theoretical principles among the non-facts in the second will seem a mistake. It may be that such principles are not obviously necessary truths, that it is possible to imagine their revision, and that they may owe their formulation at least partly to experiment or observation. But the second classification would reply that there is no clear contrast to be drawn between strictly linguistic and theoretical principles, and that all principles are vulnerable to experience and open to revision. It may be regarded as a fact that this knight is occupying b8 in the initial position, but not *just* a fact that the black knights occupy b8 and g8 in the initial position. But it is hard to see how we should decide whether the latter principle is linguistic or non-linguistic. And there is no difficulty at all in imagining that it may be revised, whether it is counted as a linguistic principle or not.

Similarly from the standpoint of the second classification the first may seem simply unrealistic. It may be said that in practice we take for granted far more in interpreting our observation than merely semantic principles. When Popper claimed that there was no such thing as neutral observation, so that in order to make sense of the instruction 'Observe' we have to assume a 'point of view' and 'theoretical problems', he was presumably thinking of more than merely semantic principles.[1] For this reason the first classification may be treated rather as an account of what scientists ought to do, than as an account of what they actually do.[2] In one way such a criticism misses the point. For the first classification is not a description of a practice at all, but rather a record of the logical status of certain claims. Nevertheless it is easy to associate a picture of an activity with the classification, in which semantic principles are first formulated, and empirical hypotheses are then proposed and finally tested in experiment or observation.

Such a picture certainly presents too simple a general account of enquiry. It is unrealistic to think of the formulation of relevant semantic principles as a preliminary to the proposal of empirical hypotheses. And once an enquiry is under way it is unrealistic to draw a sharp insulating distinction between such activities, as though the semantic principles could not change under the impact of new discoveries. Or again, in some areas of enquiry general theories may simply be applied to events in order to fit them into a pattern rather than to test the theory itself. In this respect sociologists still share certain features of historical method. Historians generally do not apply theories borrowed from economics or medicine or astronomy in order to test the theories. Rather they simply assume the theories in order to interpret the historical events. A medical view about the diagnosis of porphyria may be applied to the known facts about George III's illness, in order to establish that he was not insane. It would be very odd to treat the historical enquiry as a test of the medical diagnosis itself.[3] In the light of such practices, characteristic of normal science, it may seem wrong to accept the first classification's restriction to two determinants of belief, namely fact and language. It may seem reasonable to admit also, as the second classification does, a third category of theoretical considerations, which may not be invulnerable to facts but are assumed in interpreting what we observe.

[1] K. R. Popper, *The Logic of Scientific Discovery* (London, 1959), p. 106.
[2] See, for example, B. Barnes, *Readings in the Sociology of Science* (London, 1972), Introduction, p. 11.
[3] I. Macalpine and R. Hunter, *George III and the Mad-Business* (London, 1969).

The two classifications are plainly distinct, but it is not obvious that they are inconsistent, or that a choice has to be made between them. It is in any case more useful to be clear about their differences than to decide which of them is correct. In the light of what has so far been said the most striking difference lies in their attitudes to change. Both classifications draw a picture of certain assumed principles in contrast to their application in observation. But in the second this contrast is subordinate to the further distinction between accepting principles and questioning or revising them. The second classification contains a reference to revision, or revolutionary change, which the first entirely lacks. In the first the background principles, no doubt partly because of their association with necessary truth, are regarded as fixed and unrevisable. The second classification presents a picture of intellectual activity, while the first rather records the result of that activity in the assertion of logically distinct kinds of claim. The second presents a sociological motion picture of interaction and development, whereas the first records a still logical snapshot of the relative position of claims at some moment.

The first classification has the advantage of presenting a simple account of the logical status of claims within a formulated language. Provided that the linguistic conventions are clearly specified, its classification into necessary and contingent claims is useful. It may be helpful in an argument, within an agreed language, to clarify the sense of the terms to demonstrate a circularity or inconsistency, or to identify the exact nature of the facts in dispute. But the classification has also the deceptive clarity of the still snapshot. It tends to assume that the background linguistic principles are immune to change, or that, as in Malcolm's paper (pp. 121–7), any attempt to change them will be empty or redundant. Because of the opposition between fact and language it is easy to assume that since facts cannot be relevant to such revision there is no possibility of, or need for, it. The second classification avoids this difficulty by supposing that the revision of principles may in some way be provoked by recalcitrant facts or anomalous observations. The second classification is also closely associated with the Cartesian distinction between perfectly and imperfectly understood questions (pp. 29 and 42). In answering perfectly understood questions we are simply carrying out a 'normal' enquiry; in modifying or revising our principles we are, or may be, engaging in 'revolutionary' activities. Both classifications nevertheless accept an appeal to facts as an independent check on the formulation or acceptance of some principles. In the next section an argument will be considered which may seem to reject such an independent appeal as an illusion.

2. *Languages and cultures*

Just as the elusiveness of the term 'fact' had not been exhaustively tracked in earlier discussions, so the term 'language' still presents ambiguities. Even philosophers have used a wide range of terms to refer to the general phenomenon without always clearly distinguishing between them. They talk sometimes of conceptual schemes, of categorial frameworks, as well as of natural languages, theories and belief-systems. Some of these terms can be connected with the earlier points of distinction. A conceptual scheme, for example, may be associated with a notation-free, non-technical language identified through a set of strictly linguistic principles. In this use such a scheme would be contrasted with notation-bound natural languages and also with technical theories. A categorial framework, on the other hand, as outlined quite precisely by Körner,[1] contains principles relating to the existence of, and criteria for, the maximal categories of a system. Such a framework may differ from a conceptual scheme in its inclusion of existential claims, but, though it has links with theories and explanation, might not be regarded simply as a theory itself.

These contrasts so far treat languages primarily as impersonal constructions, such as set theory or French, which may be identified and discussed without explicit reference to the beliefs of any mathematician or French speaker. But if we extend the idea of a language to cover that of a system of beliefs, as in the case of the appeal to common sense, then this at once provides a reference to individuals or communities who hold these beliefs. Even in the case of a natural language we may refer to the 'internalised' rules assumed by its speakers as part of their belief-systems. But in associating the idea of a language with the beliefs of Jones, or of Buddhists, or of Polynesians, the idea becomes closely linked also to that of a culture or way of life. Wittgenstein's remark that 'to imagine a language is to imagine a form of life' (*Philosophical Investigations*, para. 19) clearly anticipates this extension.

Once such a step has been taken the ideas of a language and of a belief-system will attract not only logical but also historical or sociological descriptions. It is at this point, for example, that the classification of normal or revolutionary enquiries can come into play. And it is also at this point that the ideas of the social determinants of belief-systems, and of linguistic or cultural relativity, come into play. It may be argued that since all our beliefs are simply relative to the

[1] In *Categorial Frameworks*.

background language we accept, there is no possibility of objectively assessing our beliefs, and no rational basis for comparing or assessing the beliefs of others. We are then represented, as in the earlier scepticism about history, as the inevitable prisoners of our languages or cultures. In this new context, however, the situation may seem even more desperate, for the alleged relativity covers not only history but all systems of belief. The contrast between history and other disciplines which gave the earlier argument some content is here entirely lacking. We should not assume that in this case the general argument has any content at all.

Nevertheless the argument has complex ramifications. It is, for example, the basis of the anthropologists' professional reluctance to make value judgments about other cultures. It is also closely related to the so-called Sapir-Whorf hypothesis[1] which claims that the form of our languages in some way determines the fundamental beliefs that we hold. And it may simply be supported by a fashionable and crude social or material determinism, which makes us prisoners not only of antecedent beliefs, but also of prior social or material causes. The upshot, however, may be the same in all these cases. It may be said that since we cannot avoid the determining influences of our language or belief-system, we can merely accept or reject alternatives and not make any rational choice between them. On this ground there is no significant difference between a research scientist and a paranoiac. Both accept a framework of principles, in the light of which they interpret what they observe. The languages and beliefs which they accept simply determine this interpretation, and if their interpretations conflict then their assessment of each other's beliefs will simply reflect an unavoidable preference for their own. In this way, if anybody else thinks the scientist more rational than the paranoiac, then this again merely reflects their sharing of the former's but not the latter's language. If in general the former view seems preferable to some community, then it is simply that the majority of people share it.

It has already been suggested that such a position is complex and may be supported in several different ways. It may, for example, be defended by a general appeal to determinism, or to more specific differences between cognitive and value systems. The argument to be considered here, however, follows neither of these lines. It is a quite general argument which draws no special distinction between

[1] See B. L. Whorf, *Language, Thought, and Reality*, Ed. J. B. Carroll (New York, 1956). See also I. D. Currie, 'The Sapir-Whorf hypothesis' in J. E. Curtis and J. Petras (Eds.), *The Sociology of Knowledge* (London, 1970).

cognitive and value languages. But instead of appealing to a general determinism it appeals to the already mentioned myth of neutral observation. In one way this may seem to yield the sceptical conclusion quite directly. If it is a myth that observation can ever be neutral, then it may seem that observation must always be biassed in favour of some accepted background language. If the myth of neutral observation were correct, then in one way it amounts simply to the claim that our observation is always relative to a language.

But the argument makes the assumption that the term 'neutral observation' is understood in one unambiguous way, and this is not obviously so. In the premiss the appeal to the myth reflects the requirement that some linguistic resources be available for the identification of facts. In this way the premiss echoes what was earlier called a linguistic condition for such identification. But to say that we need a language in order to identify facts is not at all to say that the language simply determines how we interpret the facts. It is true that a language, like Ayer's illusion-less language from Chapter 5, may be specifically constructed to avoid reference to some phenomenon. But within its own frame of reference it still does not determine what is true or false. Nor in such a case should it be overlooked that the new language was constructed as a deviation from the everyday language in which reference to illusions is possible. In this case, as in others involving technical languages, we have a clear idea of what the alternative language is like, and may even accept both of them.

We might look at the argument from another point of view. The myth of neutral observation might be demonstrated by challenging the opposition to identify a fact totally without reference to any linguistic resources. Such a challenge cannot conceivably be met, for in one way what it demands is a reference to an inexpressible fact, that is to one which cannot be identified through a language. To try to meet such a challenge would be to approximate to the position Wittgenstein described in *Philosophical Investigations* (para. 261) as 'the point where one would like just to emit an inarticulate grunt'. Merely gesturing towards the landscape would not do in this context since it is required in order to understand such a gesture that its total ambiguity be resolved. But without the backing of some linguistic resources it would not be possible to resolve, or even perhaps strictly to talk of, ambiguity. No doubt it is possible to give ourselves some understanding of a language which cannot express certain facts; but it seems that in order to achieve this there must be a reference to another language in which those facts can be identified. In order to convince an opponent of the possibility of neutral observation it seems we would have to meet the challenge of identifying an inexpressible fact, and that seems absurd.

But the failure of such a challenge and the consequent demonstration of the myth do not show that our interpretation of what we observe is wholly determined by our language, or that we cannot compare or assess different languages, or that we are the prisoners of our conceptual scheme. For acceptance of a background language as necessary for the identification of facts is quite compatible with their independent observation in the required sense. For the independent or neutral observation required is not observation without linguistic resources, but only observation describable in terms which falsify our beliefs. The point is the same as that made earlier (Chapter 4, pp. 75-7) about the limited determining power of a background language. The language may determine what we look for, but it does not follow that it determines what we find. To accept neutral observation as a myth in the present context is to place a limit on our ability to recognise certain facts, but it is not to concede that everything we observe is determined by our language. The difference between a scientist and a paranoiac is that the former, but not the latter, can be surprised.

Equally the myth of neutral observation in this version does not entail that we are prisoners of our background language. No doubt many people much of the time are content with 'normal' activity and do not stop to question their background assumptions. Perhaps some really become incapable of such questioning, but if so this is an additional hazard which does not necessarily attach merely to the acceptance of a language. It has been suggested that our language may place, or mark, restrictions on what we recognise in observation, but this by itself does not show that these restrictions are immovable. On the contrary we may be impressed by the idea of such restrictions just because we can offer historical illustrations of languages which could not express facts which we now recognise. But such illustrations demonstrate the removal of barriers and not their insurmountability.

Yet the illustration points to our own unrecognised limitations. If a language at any time is limited in this way, then our own language is also limited. We may become obsessed with the idea that we cannot break out of our background framework just because we cannot anticipate or recognise our own limitations. It may be imagined, then, that there are certain elements in our language or system of belief which simply cannot be changed, and which consequently imprison us. But the argument is again unsound. Even if it is true that we cannot dispense completely with, or totally reject, linguistic resources, it does not follow that there are any particular items in the language which are indispensable. It may be that although we cannot intelligibly abandon all our linguistic principles nevertheless any of them separately could be rejected. But in that case again the restrictive power of language in this argument amounts only to the claim that some language is necessary, and not that any particular form of language is necessary. The restrictions which the argument imposes are not in any specific case irremovable.

It is partly in this way that ordinary language may be cast in the role of an ultimately indispensable resource. For certainly we may see technical theories as developing out of, and away from, cruder common-sense ideas. The restrictions of a technical language may naturally be measured against the richer and less exact terms of colloquial discourse from which it developed. In addition it may even be argued that ordinary language is in some way complete, so that it already contains every possible idea. But such a position is incoherent, for it describes ordinary language in two incompatible ways. On one side it is supposed that everything that can be expressed at all can be expressed in ordinary language, while on the other it is assumed that ordinary language is to be precisely contrasted with other technical systems. If the first account is accepted then the argument simply expresses again the general myth of neutral observation and the requirement of some linguistic resources in identifying facts. If the second account is accepted, then ordinary language is not an indispensable resource, or an immovable barrier, just because it is contrasted with technical theories which have removed such barriers and dispensed with its resources.

Such arguments fail, but they may help to provide some answer to the question raised in Chapter 1 about the persistent appeal to ordinary language or common sense in philosophy. No doubt the answer is complex. Partly it may be that ordinary language is more accessible than any technical system. Partly it may be because of some ambiguity in the notion of a language itself, which encourages the belief in a realm of ordinary language meanings available exclusively to philosophers. Partly, too, it reflects the creditable desire to limit philosophical extravagance. But partly it is, as these arguments suggest, because of a belief in the fundamental and unchangeable status of ordinary language. Certainly if we require a language from which to view the limitations of another, then ordinary language is a natural resource against which to measure the limitations of technical theories. But such an argument does not establish any priority in ordinary language over its technical rivals. On the contrary it shows that the two kinds of language are symmetrically related; either may be viewed from the standpoint of the other. Ordinary language may have historical priority, but the argument establishes nothing more than that.

In the first chapter an obvious distinction was drawn between describing and recommending methods. The argument here has been mainly descriptive and critical of some recent aims and methods in philosophy but it is scarcely possible to divorce such an argument completely from recommendation. If the argument is at all sound, then recent philosophy has in some respects fallen foul of the complexities and ambiguities inherent in the term 'language'. What has been undertaken here is only an attempt to uncover the surface layers of this complex term, or again to indicate rather than explore the interconnections between different branches of the whole family. But further tasks of elucidation in this area still remain, for philosophers as for other theorists. Plainly more needs to be said both of the general idea of a language, and also of the detailed connections between items in any particular language. These tasks have been only indicated here and not carried out, but something has been said of their status. In particular it has been suggested that they cannot usefully be classified as exclusively linguistic or factual. In the field of natural language, for example, psychologists and linguists contribute to their elucidation as well as philosophers. If the account given here is correct, then there is no justification for an exclusive separation of philosophical and non-philosophical interests in this or any other case. Specifically there is no good reason to think of one kind of enquiry as exclusively factual and of the other as exclusively non-factual.

Nevertheless to recommend philosophers to direct their enquiries more consciously towards those of other disciplines may be misleading. It may suggest, what is not true, that philosophers in recent times have totally misdirected their enquiries. Some philosophers, indeed, have taken such a view,[1] but the position is less straightforward than this suggests. The dominant interest in language throughout the philosophical revolution was not simply a curious aberration. It was prompted by developments in logic and linguistic studies,

[1] C. W. K. Mundle, for example, in *A Critique of Linguistic Philosophy* (p. 263) takes the view that by the end of the century 'the Linguistic Revolution in Philosophy will . . . be recognised . . . as one of the most curious curios in the history of ideas'. He also, more plausibly, makes a plea for a less exclusive philosophy.

just as seventeenth-century philosophy was prompted by developments in mathematics and physics. What seems to have been distorted is not so much what philosophers have been doing as what they have said that they have been doing. What seems to be unjustified is less their practice than their theory.

The point can be illustrated by reference to one problem, noted earlier (Chapter 4, pp. 70–72), about G. E. Moore's kind of analysis. In one way Moore's account of analysis committed him to a realm of concepts or propositions to be analysed independently of the words of any natural language. It was for this reason that he wished to distinguish his own kind of analysis from the work of lexicographers. It has been suggested that such a view of analysis can be seriously misleading, if the idea of independence from a natural or notation-bound language is not fully understood. It would, for example, plainly be impossible for Moore ever to get an analysis started without some reference to an expression whose meaning was to be analysed. Although officially the analysis was independent of the expressions of any natural language, in practice some such expressions had to be used. Certainly it would be hard to deny that often Moore's analyses were extremely valuable; but his own account of analysis, as he himself conceded, was never satisfactory.

In a similar way it is at least possible that philosophical practice in recent times has not, even could not have, matched the theory that went with it. Whether an argument or point of view has implications outside philosophy, or whether it is of exclusively philosophical interest, is after all not settled merely by the beliefs of its author. Certainly the best work of linguistic philosophers has been related to the general elucidation of natural language and of natural language meaning. In the case of some philosophers, Austin for example, the work was specifically undertaken for the sake of a joint enterprise with other disciplines. If the elucidation of terms cannot entirely be separated from the practices of other first-order disciplines, then it is inevitable that philosophical accounts of these terms have a bearing on other disciplines, whether this is recognised or not. What in this case seems wrong is less the philosophical activity of elucidation than the philosophical theory that was attached to it, the theory that philosophical analysis, since it is linguistic and non-factual, has no conceivable bearing on any substantive enquiry, that it is exclusively philosophical.

It is perhaps not surprising that linguistic philosophy might have some bearing on other enquiries into language. It may still be doubted whether a similar overlap is to be expected or found in other areas.

Yet if the general point is correct it will hold for other areas of philosophy and the corresponding non-philosophical disciplines as well. It has in any case already been suggested (Chapter 7, pp. 132–3) that the philosophical interest in meaning is not simply due to the subject-matter but to the nature of the theoretical problems in it. If such theoretical problems arise in other areas there is no reason why they similarly should not be the subject of philosophical enquiry. If questions of meaning arise within these non-philosophical contexts, and if they cannot be entirely separated from questions about the constitutive principles in the area, then they will define a point of overlap with philosophy. Philosophical claims about mind, or the law, or morality may in this way relate quite directly to psychologists' theories, or legal codes, or moral practices and beliefs. In the area of morality, for example, about which regrettably little has so far been said, there seems no special merit in regarding utilitarianism as a substantive moral theory rather than as a linguistic proposal of criteria for the application of moral terms. Equally the criticism, refinement, or even rejection of utilitarian principles and criteria might just as well be understood in either of these ways. In general such connections may arise either at the level of articulating the general structure of a language or theory, or from the more specific task of mapping detailed relations between terms in some particular language or theory. Although recent philosophers have generally expressed their activities in terms of linguistic or conceptual enquiry, they have nevertheless carried out tasks of just these kinds.

Such points as these might be summarised in a general recommendation to return to something like the pre-revolutionary Cartesian picture of Chapter 2. Of course, it is not now possible to return to the state of innocence in which the picture was originally painted; nor can the picture be accepted in its entirety any more than its rival can. In Descartes' version too great an emphasis was certainly placed on a mathematical model of enquiry. And in the version due to his successors the idea of a total system embracing every area of enquiry and belief is too unclear to be taken seriously. On the other side it is not now possible to disregard the revolutionary virtues which Descartes overlooked. The revolutionary insistence on the importance of language, and the exploration of intellectual pathology in the production of meaningless or empty questions, are necessary additions to be made to the Cartesian scheme. But in his insistence on a close connection between philosophy and science, and in his location of areas of enquiry common to philosophy and other disciplines, Descartes was nearer the truth than some revolutionaries.

BIBLIOGRAPHY

The bibliography lists books and articles related to the text by chapter. Under (A) are listed items referred to in the text; under (B) are listed some suggestions for further reading.

CHAPTER 1: THE REVOLUTIONARY BACKGROUND

(A)

A. J. Ayer (1) *et al.*, *The Revolution in Philosophy* (London, 1956)

Y. Bar-Hillel, 'Carnap's Logical Syntax of Language' in P. Schilpp (Ed.) *The Philosophy of R. Carnap* (La Salle, 1963)

I. Berlin (Ed.), *The Age of Enlightenment* (New York, 1956)

R. Carnap (1), *Logical Syntax of Language* (London, 1937)

E. Gellner, *Words and Things* (London, 1959)

D. Hume, *An Enquiry concerning Human Understanding* (London, 1777)

I. Kant, *Prolegomena to any Future Metaphysics*, Tr. and Ed. L. W. Beck (New York, 1950)

C. W. K. Mundle (1), *A Critique of Linguistic Philosophy* (Oxford, 1970)

R. S. Peters, *Ethics and Education* (London, 1966)

W. V. O. Quine (1), *Mathematical Logic* (Harvard, 1940)

H. Reichenbach, *The Rise of Scientific Philosophy* (California, 1951)

B. Russell (1), *The Principles of Mathematics* (2nd ed., London, 1937)

J. Searle (1), *Speech Acts* (Cambridge, 1969)

P. F. Strawson (1), 'Construction and Analysis' in A. J. Ayer (1)

J. O. Urmson, *Philosophical Analysis* (Oxford, 1956)

G. J. Warnock, *English Philosophy since 1900* (Oxford, 1963)

(B)

Logical positivism

A. J. Ayer (2) (Ed.), *Logical Positivism* (New York, 1959)

A. J. Ayer (3), *Language, Truth, and Logic* (2nd ed., London, 1946)

P. Achinstein and S. F. Barker (Eds.), *The Legacy of Logical Positivism* (Baltimore, 1969)

Linguistic philosophy, see Chapter 7

J. L. Austin (1), *Philosophical Papers* (Oxford, 1961)
F. Waismann, *The Principles of Linguistic Philosophy*, Ed. R. Harré (London, 1965)
J. Wisdom, *Philosophy and Psycho-Analysis* (Oxford, 1953)
L. Wittgenstein (1), *Blue and Brown Books* (Oxford, 1958)
L. Wittgenstein (2), *Philosophical Investigations* (Oxford, 1953)

Criticisms of linguistic philosophy

S. Hampshire, S. Körner and A. Duncan-Jones (1), 'Are all Philosophical Questions Questions of Language?', *PASSV*, 1948
H. H. Price, 'Clarity is not Enough', *PASSV*, 1945
B. Russell (2), 'The Cult of Common Usage', *British Journal for the Philosophy of Science*, 1953

General surveys

H. D. Lewis (Ed.), *Contemporary British Philosophy* (3rd ser., London, 1956)
C. A. Mace (Ed.), *British Philosophy in the Mid-Century* (London, 1957)
R. Rorty (Ed.), *The Linguistic Turn* (Chicago, 1967)

CHAPTER 2: PHILOSOPHY AND SCIENCE

(A)

R. Descartes, *Rules for the Direction of the Mind*, Tr. and Ed. E. S. Haldane and G. R. T. Ross in *Works*, vol. I (Cambridge, 1911)
J. S. Haldane, *The Sciences and Philosophy* (London, 1929)
I. Kant (2), *The Critique of Pure Reason*, Tr. N. Kemp Smith (London 1929)
T. S. Kuhn, *The Structure of Scientific Revolutions* (Chicago, 1966)
M. Schlick, 'The Future of Philosophy' in R. Rorty (Ed.) *The Linguistic Turn*, see Chapter 1(B)
H. Sidgwick, *Philosophy: Its Scope and Relations* (London, 1902)
F. Waismann, *The Principles of Linguistic Philosophy*, see Chapter 1(B)
L. Wittgenstein (3), *Tractatus Logico-Philosophicus*, Tr. D. Pears and B. Mc-Guinness (London, 1961)

(B)

Philosophy and science

A. J. Ayer (4), 'Philosophy and Science' in *Metaphysics and Common Sense* (London, 1969)
I. Lakatos and A. Musgrave (Eds.), *Criticism and the Growth of Knowledge* (Cambridge, 1970)
S. Körner (2), *Experience and Theory* (London, 1966)
K. R. Popper, *The Logic of Scientific Discovery* (London, 1959)

Austin and Wittgenstein

S. Cavell, S. Hampshire, J. O. Urmson, G. J. Warnock, articles in R. Rorty (Ed.) *The Linguistic Turn*, see Chapter 1(B)

M. Furberg, *Saying and Meaning* (Oxford, 1971)
G. Pitcher (Ed.), *Wittgenstein: The Philosophical Investigations* (London, 1968)

CHAPTER 3: PHILOSOPHY AND HISTORY

(A)

S. Körner (3), *Fundamental Questions in Philosophy* (London, 1971)
W. H. Walsh, *An Introduction to Philosophy of History* (London, 1951)

(B)

W. H. Dray, *Philosophy of History* (New Jersey, 1964)
P. Gardiner (Ed.), *Theories of History* (Glencoe, 1959)
L. I. Krimerman (Ed.), *The Nature and Scope of Social Science* (New York, 1969)
P. Winch, *The Idea of a Social Science* (London, 1958)

CHAPTER 4: FACT AND LANGUAGE

(A)

G. E. M. Anscombe, 'On Brute Facts', *Analysis*, 1958
A. J. Ayer (5), 'Philosophy and Language' in *The Concept of a Person* (London 1964)
J. A. Bernadete, 'Sense-perception and the *A Priori*', *Mind*, 1969
R. M. Chisholm, *Theory of Knowledge* (New Jersey, 1966)
S. Körner (4), *Categorial Frameworks* (Oxford, 1970)
G. E. Moore (1), *Principia Ethica* (Cambridge, 1903)
A. Pap, *The A Priori in Physical Theory* (New York, 1946)
W. V. O. Quine (2), 'Two Dogmas of Empiricism' in *From a Logical Point of View* (2nd ed., Harvard, 1964)
W. V. O. Quine (3), *The Philosophy of Logic* (New Jersey, 1969)
J. Rawls, 'Two Concepts of Rules', *Philosophical Review*, 1955
M. Schlick, 'The Future of Philosophy', *see* Chapter 2(A)
J. Searle (2), 'How to Derive "Ought" from "Is"', *Philosophical Review*, 1964
A. White, *G. E. Moore* (Oxford, 1958)
J. Wisdom, *Philosophy and Psycho-Analysis*, *see* Chapter 1(B)

(B)

The analytic/synthetic distinction

R. Hall, 'A Bibliography', *Philosophical Quarterly*, 1966

Philosophy and Linguistics, see Chapter 7(B)

Janet Fodor, 'Formal Linguistics and Formal Logic' in J. Lyons (Ed.), *New Horizons in Linguistics* (London, 1970)
C. Lyas (Ed.), *Philosophy and Linguistics* (London, 1971)
P. Ziff, *Semantic Analysis* (New York, 1960)

Philosophy and Chomsky

N. Chomsky (1), *Language and Mind* (New York, 1968)
N. Chomsky (2), 'Recent Contributions to the Theory of Innate Ideas', *Synthese*, 1967

N. Goodman (1), 'The Epistemological Argument', *Synthese*, 1967
H. Putnam, 'The "Innateness Hypothesis" and Explanatory Models in Linguistics', *Synthese,* 1967

Languages and theories

R. Carnap (2), 'The Methodological Character of Theoretical Concepts' in Feigl, Scriven and Maxwell (Eds.), *Minnesota Studies in the Philosophy of Science*, vol. I, (Minneapolis, 1958)
N. R. Hanson, *Patterns of Discovery* (Cambridge, 1958)
M. Hesse, 'Is There an Independent Observation Language?' in R. G. Colodny (Ed.), *The Nature and Function of Scientific Theories* (Pittsburgh, 1970)
T. S. Kuhn, *The Structure of Scientific Revolutions, see* Chapter 2(A)

CHAPTER 5: LANGUAGE AND PERCEPTION

(A)

J. L. Austin (2), *Sense and Sensibilia* (Oxford, 1962)
A. J. Ayer (6), *The Foundations of Empirical Knowledge* (London, 1940)
A. J. Ayer (7), *The Origins of Pragmatism* (London, 1968)
C. W. K. Mundle (2), *Perception: Facts and Theories* (Oxford, 1971)

(B)

A. J. Ayer (8), 'Phenomenalism', *PAS*, 1950
A. J. Ayer (9), 'Has Austin Refuted the Sense-Datum Theory?', *Synthese*, 1967
R. G. Collingwood, *An Essay on Philosophical Method* (Oxford, 1933)
N. Goodman (2), *The Structure of Appearance* (Harvard, 1951)
G. A. Paul, 'Is There a Problem about Sense-Data?', *PASSV* 1936, reprinted in A. G. N. Flew (Ed.), *Logic and Language* (1st ser., Oxford, 1951)
H. H. Price, *Perception* (London, 1932)

CHAPTER 6: SCEPTICISM

(A)

J. L. Austin (1), *Philosophical Papers, see* Chapter 1(B)
R. Carnap (3), *Logical Foundations of Probability* (Chicago, 1950)
N. Goodman (2), *The Structure of Appearance, see* Chapter 5(B)
C. Hempel, *Aspects of Scientific Explanation* (New York, 1965)
S. Körner (4), *Categorial Frameworks, see* Chapter 4(A)
J. Locke, *An Essay concerning Human Understanding*, Ed. A. C. Fraser (Oxford, 1894)
W. G. Lycan, 'Non-inductive Evidence', *American Philosophical Quarterly*, 1971
D. E. Morrison and R. E. Henkel (Eds.), *The Significance Test Controversy* (London, 1970)
R. W. Newell, *The Concept of Philosophy* (London, 1967)
J. Wisdom, *Philosophy and Psycho-Analysis, see* Chapter 1(B)

(B)

A. J. Ayer (10), *Philosophical Essays* (London, 1954)
A. J. Ayer (11), 'Philosophical Scepticism' in H. D. Lewis (Ed.), *Contemporary British Philosophy, see* Chapter 1(B)

A. G. N. Flew (Ed.), *Logic and Language* (1st ser., Oxford, 1951)
G. E. Moore (2), 'A Proof of an External World', and 'A Defence of Common Sense' in *Philosophical Papers* (London, 1959)
P. F. Strawson (2), *Individuals* (London, 1959)

CHAPTER 7: ORDINARY LANGUAGE

(A)

J. L. Austin (1), *Philosophical Papers, see* Chapter 1(B)
J. L. Austin (3), *How to Do Things with Words* (Oxford, 1962)
N. Malcolm, 'Moore and Ordinary Language' in P. Schilpp (Ed.), *The Philosophy of G. E. Moore* (Evanston and Chicago, 1942). Reprinted in R. Rorty (Ed.), *see* Chapter 1(B)
B. Russell, 'On Denoting', *Mind*, 1905. Reprinted in R. C. Marsh (Ed.), *Logic and Knowledge* (London, 1956)
J. Searle (1), *Speech Acts, see* Chapter 1(A)
P. F. Strawson (2), *Individuals, see* Chapter 6(B)
P. F. Strawson (3), 'On Referring', *Mind*, 1950
P. F. Strawson (4), *Introduction to Logical Theory* (London, 1952)
G. J. Warnock, *English Philosophy since* 1900, *see* Chapter 1(A)
L. Wittgenstein (2), *Philosophical Investigations, see* Chapter 1(B)
L. Wittgenstein (3), *Tractatus Logico-Philosophicus, see* Chapter 2(A)

(B)

Ordinary language as an arbiter, see Chapter 1(B)

H. G. Alexander, H. S. Eveling and G. O. M. Leith, A. G. N. Flew (2), R. Harré, J. W. N. Watkins, articles on the Paradigm Case Argument, *Analysis*, 1957–8
E. Gellner, *Words and Things, see* Chapter 1(A)
J. Passmore, 'Professor Ryle's use of "use" and "usage" ', *Philosophical Review*, 1954
G. Ryle, 'Ordinary Language', *Philosophical Review*, 1953

Ordinary language and linguistics

C. J. Fillmore, 'Types of Lexical Information' in F. Kiefer (Ed.), *Studies in Syntax and Semantics* (Dordrecht, 1969)
J. Katz, *The Philosophy of Language* (New York, 1966)
C. Lyas (Ed.), *Philosophy and Linguistics, see* Chapter 4(B)
W. V. O. Quine (4), *Word and Object* (Massachusetts, 1960)
P. Ziff, *Semantic Analysis, see* Chapter 4(B)

CHAPTER 8: CONCEPTUAL SCHEMES AND CATEGORIAL FRAMEWORKS

(A)

B. Barnes (Ed.), *Readings in the Sociology of Science* (London, 1972)
I. D. Currie, 'The Sapir-Whorf Hypothesis' in J. E. Curtis and J. Petras (Eds.), *The Sociology of Knowledge* (London, 1970)
S. Körner (4), *Categorial Frameworks, see* Chapter 4(A)

I. Macalpine and R. Hunter, *George III and the Mad-Business* (London, 1969)
C. W. K. Mundle (1), *A Critique of Linguistic Philosophy, see* Chapter 1(A)
K. R. Popper, *The Logic of Scientific Discovery, see* Chapter 2(B)
B. L. Whorf, *Language, Thought and Reality,* Ed. J. B. Carroll (New York, 1956)
L. Wittgenstein (2), *Philosophical Investigations, see* Chapter 1(B)

(B)

D. Davidson and J. Hintikka (Eds.), *Words and Objections: essays on the work of W. V. O. Quine* (Dordrecht, 1969)
W. V. O. Quine and J. S. Ullian, *The Web of Belief* (New York, 1970)

INDEX